Scott Carley's *Can I Trust You* is a game-changer for anyone navigating the complex world of business relationships. I had the privilege of meeting Scott through a business networking group in Austin, and his innovative ‹Trust Credit Score™› framework immediately resonated with me. At a pivotal moment in my career transition, Scott's methodologies helped me uncover my unique advantages by identifying how others perceive my strengths and trustworthiness.

What truly set Scott's approach apart was how practical and actionable it proved to be. As I evaluated new career opportunities and interviewed, I used the Trust Credit Score™ framework to assess not only how I was perceived, but also the trust dynamics within each organization. This gave me a clear, objective way to determine which company's culture and leadership aligned with my values and where I could thrive. The Trust Credit Score™ became an invaluable tool in choosing the right fit for my next professional chapter. By applying his principles, I've experienced firsthand how elevated trust accelerates collaboration and opens doors to new opportunities.

Can I Trust You is a must-read for leaders, teams, and professionals seeking to enhance their performance and relationships. Scott's wisdom will inspire you to build trust intentionally, creating lasting impact in both your career and personal life.

—**Lucie Wuescher,** Risk Advisory Principal,
Baker Tilly

In today's world, trust is the unseen catalyst that can either accelerate or stagnate success. Scott Carley's formula, the Trust Credit Score™ System offers a transformative method to maximize and amplify trust, similar to how a FICO score revolutionizes financial credibility. By recognizing trust as a non-negotiable and essential ingredient to both personal and business results, this system empowers organizations to adopt cooperation, drive innovation, and achieve unprecedented success. I invite you to learn this framework and unlock your potential!

—**Amy Lemire**, CSP DTM AIM Training & Consulting

Scott Carley delivers a game-changing framework that turns trust into a measurable, actionable asset. The Trust Credit Score™ System gives leaders and teams a clear path to stronger relationships, faster results, and real business growth. If trust matters in your world, this book belongs on your desk—now.

—**Susan Friedmann**, CSP, international bestselling author of *Riches in Niches: How to Make it BIG in a small Market*

Trust is the foundation of life, from our family, our friends, and of course our business. Scott Carley takes a topic that we assume is a "given" and shows us its absolute necessity in our work environment. Through his book, *Can I Trust You*, we see the cost of low trust and the huge benefits of high trust. Thank you Scott for reminding us all that "trust" can't be taken for granted.

—**Holly Prescott**, Certified Life Coach and Keller Williams Realty franchise owner

ENDORSEMENTS

The Trust Credit Score™ is one of those ideas that makes you stop and say, 'Why hasn't anyone done this before?' Scott Carley has distilled a lifetime of leadership wisdom into a simple, powerful framework every business leader needs to understand. I've known Scott for over a decade, and this book is the culmination of the insight, integrity, and authenticity he brings to every room. Trust is the currency of leadership—and this is your credit report.

—**Jeff Kikel,** Author of *The Business Owner Retirement Blueprint* and Founder of Sure Horizon Retirement Advisors

In *Can I Trust You*, Scott Carley illuminates the power of trust as the marching orders we give our mind whenever we interact with other humans. You get powerful tools to increase your trust score solidly grounded in proven psychological principles with an authentic personal perspective and immediately practical applications.

—**Paul H. Jenkins, Ph.D.,** Psychologist and Author of *Pathological Positivity*

What a great concept, 'Your Trust Rating!' We all know that Trust is the oil of cooperation. Without it everything is restricted and with it, all is possible. I applaud my amazing colleague Scott Carley for articulating this concept so well and showing us how to increase trust in all that we do. Make this book your daily guide!

—**Jim Cathcart,** CSP, CPAE Mentor to Experts and author of *Relationship Selling.*

In *Can I Trust You*, Scott Carley turns this phrase into a magnifying glass for a wake-up call for leaders everywhere. If you're losing time, traction or top talent and can't quite put your finger on why—start here. With piercing clarity and practical insight, it uncovers the invisible cost of fractured trust and charts a powerful path to rebuild it. Whether you're leading a start-up or a seasoned team, these pages offer the wisdom, urgency and tools you need to restore alignment, reengage your people and lead with integrity. A must-read for leaders who refuse to settle for dysfunction.

—**Randy Phillips,** Pastor of LifeFamily Churches,
Founder of Phillips, Craig & Dean

This book is a must-read go to guide for leaders wanting to learn a strategic and effective system to cultivate a high-trust, high-results culture!

—**Judy Kay Mausolf,** Dental Culturalist,
Speaker, Published Author

Can I Trust You? and *The Trust Credit Score*™ is a great tool for anyone who is responsible for leading a team. It provided me with valuable insights into navigating my team dynamics, especially when a team is struggling or is experiencing changes in membership. Using the credit score, it is easy to identify the issues with team dynamics and develop actionable steps to rebuild trust and strengthen the team to be more productive.

—**Renee Acosta,** Senior Associate Dean for Academic Affairs,
University of Texas College of Pharmacy

Can I Trust You, Scott Carley, known as The Change Energizer, introduces a groundbreaking framework that redefines how trust is measured and cultivated within organizations. Drawing a compelling parallel to the FICO credit score, Carley's Trust Credit Score™ quantifies trustworthiness, revealing its profound impact on team dynamics, sales and financial performance. This concise yet insightful book offers a practical roadmap for individuals and businesses to assess and elevate trust, unlocking faster cooperation and greater success.

The book shines in its real-world applications, particularly in illustrating how high trust accelerates decision-making, boosts sales and reduces operational costs, while low trust creates friction and financial losses.

Overall, *Can I Trust You*, is a must-read for leaders, teams, and sales professionals seeking to foster collaboration and drive results. Carley's innovative approach transforms an intangible concept into a measurable asset, offering a clear path to enhanced performance and profitability.

—**John Prescott**, Operating Partner /
KWU Master Faculty / FES Instructor

"Can I Trust You?" isn't just theory, Scott Carley has lived every word. I've witnessed his journey of redemption and leadership firsthand, and this book distills that hard-earned wisdom into a powerful, practical guide for rebuilding trust in life and business.

—**Michelle Villalobos**, MBA, CSP

Scott Carley has a gift for helping leaders see what's happening beneath the surface - especially when it comes to trust. He's spent years helping leadership teams navigate tough transitions, misalignment and broken communication and his Trust Credit Score model gives language to what many of us have sensed but struggled to articulate.

I've seen Scott in action as a dynamic keynote speaker, engaging facilitator and servant leader. Having collaborated with Scott through the National Speakers Association, I've witnessed firsthand his unparalleled ability to energize and guide leaders through transformative change. His insights are not only profound but also actionable, making complex trust dynamics accessible and manageable. He leads with energy, but more importantly, with clarity and conviction. His approach invites leaders to take ownership, rebuild credibility and create momentum in their teams. If you've ever felt like something in your leadership culture was "off" but couldn't quite name it, Scott's work will help you connect the dots.

This book is more than just a read; it's a roadmap for leaders committed to cultivating authentic relationships and fostering environments where trust thrives. Scott's approach is both enlightening and empowering, making Can I Trust You? an indispensable resource for any leader aiming to navigate the intricacies of trust in today's business landscape.

—**Kara D. Kelley,** SHRM-SCP, SPHR CEO,
Clinical HR | Past President, NSA Austin

The Trust Credit Score™! What a great lens for leaders to use when evaluating why they have high or low trust for someone. Instead of having just an overall "gut feeling" of high or low trust for a person, Scott Carley's book *Can I Trust You?* provides a framework to evaluate that feeling. For leaders and managers, this can be a game-changer when providing constructive feedback to help your employees improve! Additionally, I like that this book gives practical ways broken trust can begin to be rebuilt.

—**Kymberli S.J. Speight,** Keynote Speaker,
Author, Workshop Facilitator

Scott Carley has his finger on the pulse of organizational leadership...and it's all about trust! From the first chapter to the last, you will find this book essential for gaining traction in your organization. Scott not only accurately describes the downfall of leaders who have broken trust with people, but also how to build up your trust to develop high functioning, goal accomplishing teams. I highly recommend this book to anyone looking to develop their personal leadership skills and move teams forward.

—**Scott Vermillion**, President of
Yellow Bee Marketing

As a combat veteran with 24 years of service across the full spectrum of military operations from enabling Special Operations Forces to leading strategic cyberspace initiatives, I've come to understand one universal truth: trust is the foundation upon which all high-performing teams are built. In environments where failure is not an option, trust isn't a soft skill, it's a mission-critical asset.

That's why *The Trust Credit Score*™ by Scott Carley immediately resonated with me. Scott has captured the intangible essence of trust and made it measurable, actionable, scalable and practical. His framework doesn't just provide a new way of thinking; it offers a effective system for leaders who must operate with precision and integrity in dynamic, high-pressure environments.

Scott's insights mirror the very principles that drive elite teams to success; transparency, accountability, and consistent behavior. Just as I've seen trust either enable or erode battlefield cohesion, Scott shows how trust accelerates or stalls business performance. His methodology for measuring and rebuilding trust is not only timely, it's essential for leaders committed to growth, collaboration, and sustained excellence.

I trust Scott Carley, not just because of his friendship, but because of his unwavering commitment to empowering others. The Trust Credit Score™ is a game-changer, and I recommend it without hesitation to anyone who values performance, purpose, and people.

—**Austin Boone,** CW4 (Ret.), U.S. Army

CAN I TRUST YOU?

The Silent Question
Everyone in Business Is Asking

SCOTT CARLEY

The Trust Energizer™

First Edition
Printed in the United States of America
Aurell Publishers
ISBN: 979-8-9986864-0-5

For more information or to book a keynote, workshop, or certification training, visit: **CallTheEnergizer.com**

Dedication

To my wife, Carol — for your steady love
and support through every chapter.

To Malori and Maesan — for riding the roller coaster
of your dad's journey back to influence.

To Dylan, Morgan, and Lauren — thanks for welcoming me
in and sharing your mom with Pops.

And to the business community across the country
who've taken the journey with me to build high-level,
influential trust in leadership and life.

This book is for those who know that trust isn't given —
it's loaned, earned, rebuilt and lived out every day.

CONTENTS

Foreword. . . . . *xix*

PART I:
THE FOUNDATION OF TRUST

1. An Executive Summary. **3**

Overview of the Trust Credit Score concept, its importance, and the benefits of improving trust in personal and professional life.

2. Trust – Your Ultimate X-Factor **13**

Explore why trust is the critical factor for success, growth, and cooperation in any relationship or team.

3. Trust on Credit: Trust Isn't Free – It's a Loan **21**

Introduce the concept that trust is earned incrementally and can be borrowed or lost based on actions.

PART II:
THE FIVE SCORES OF TRUST

4. The First Score: Their Vibe Is On Point –
Appearance and Body Language **31**

The first impression's power and how body language and appearance communicate trustworthiness.

5. The Second Score: They Are Straight Up Solid – Motives and Agenda .41

Evaluating honesty, transparency, and consistency of motives.

6. The Third Score: We're On The Same Page – Integrity and Congruence. 49

The importance of aligning values, words, and actions to establish deeper trust.

7. The Fourth Score They Are Built For This – Expertise and Skillset 57

Why expertise and capability play a key role in building trust.

8. The Fifth Score: They've Got Receipts – Your Track Record .67

How past results and consistency validate trustworthiness.

PART III:
APPLYING THE TRUST CREDIT SCORE

9. Why CEO's Want To Use the Trust Credit Score. . .77

Why CEOs and senior leaders should integrate the Trust Credit Score to enhance team performance, drive collaboration, and build organizational credibility.

Focus on high-level applications such as fostering trust across teams, improving customer relationships, and addressing fractured trust within the organization.

10. Using Disney's "Casting-Call" for Hiring 85

How Disney's approach to hiring and role alignment parallels building trust in teams.

11. How to Score a Trust Crash 89

Identifying and measuring trust failures to pave the way for recovery.

12. How to Have a Courageous Conversation 99

Addressing trust fractures through honest, empathetic dialogue.

13. The Significance of Two Perspectives of Trust (Crash vs Credit) .113

Explaining the dual lens of trust: earning it and recovering from a breach.

14. How to Use the Two-Perspective Model 119

Practical applications of viewing trust through these two perspectives in leadership and relationships.

PART IV:
BEYOND THE WORKPLACE

15. Reputation Rehab 127

How to rebuild trust at work and in life.

16. How to Rebuild Trust Within the Family 137

How trust scores apply to family dynamics and improving personal relationships.

17. TCS is *Not a Weapon* **141**

Emphasizing the importance of using the Trust Credit Score as a tool for growth, not manipulation or harm.

PART V:
TRUST THAT LASTS

18. The Trust Credit Score™ –
Your New Culture Code **147**

About the Author **153**

FOREWORD

Can I Trust You?

"Help! Help! Help!"

My introduction into long term care started with a tour of the nursing home I would eventually call home for the first two years of my career. We started the tour on the 5th floor, then took the stairs to the 4th floor, skipped the 3rd, being assured it looked exactly like the 4th and the 5th and landed on the 2nd floor. The 2nd floor had recently been transformed from a long term care unit, to a short term care unit. It was like walking into a completely different center, with bright lights, restaurant style dining room and a state of the art rehabilitation center.

The first time I ever stepped foot on the 3rd floor, however, was a few weeks later, after going through the hiring process and two days of orientation, I began to walk around and explore. As promised, the 3rd floor looked exactly like the 4th and 5th floors, with one small exception; the residents on the 3rd floor needed a lot more attention. It was what they called, the skilled unit.

The center is shaped like a figure eight, with two elevators in the middle opening up in front of the nurses station. Semi-private resident rooms spread out on either side, with a dining area on one end and a sitting area on the other. I introduced myself to the nurse sitting behind the desk on my first visit. Her name was Donna, had brown shoulder length hair and wore a white lab coat over her scrubs. She was the unit manager. She stood up to shake my hand and welcome me aboard when I walked up. Then it happened.

"Help! Help! Help!" a woman cried out. Startled, I took a step backward and looked toward the sound. Donna didn't flinch. In fact, she never took her eyes off me.

"I'm right here," she called out. She checked her pockets, then gave me a final smile as she walked out of the nurses station. "I'll be right back," she said. "Don't go anywhere." I nodded, tight lipped. Donna walked to a residents room, knocked lightly on a partially opened door and went in. "I'm here. I'm here," she said.

A few minutes later, Donna came out and went to the

kitchenette. She held up a finger, letting me know she needed another minute. I nodded. Inside the kitchenette she grabbed a small can of ginger ale, a straw and an ice cream cone. She held them up for my view as she went back into the residents room.

"That is Mrs. Andrews," she said, coming back to the nurses station. "She's blind. She lost her eyesight due to complications from diabetes a few months ago." I exhaled loudly. She nodded. "I know. Scary." She went back behind the nurses station and sat down.

We spent the next 20 minutes or so talking, I told her all about me and my experience working at a military clinic and she told me all about her and her experience working in long term care.

"People only come here for one reason," she said. "Do you know what it is?" I looked away, thinking about it and shrugged.

"Not really."

"A promise," she said. "A promise. That is why people come here. That is why family members bring their loved ones here. They want a promise that everything is going to be okay. A promise that they can trust us. A promise that they will be safe." I nodded.

"Wow. Right. Okay. That makes sense," I said.

"I want you to keep that in mind as you walk around and interact with some of the residents. Any time you get a chance, assure them that they are okay. Assure them that this is a safe place. Ask them if they need anything, and if they say yes, get it for them, or get one of us and we will get it for them." I nodded.

"Got it," I said.

That conversation happened more than 20 years ago—and it remains one of the most important lessons I've ever learned: in senior care, trust is everything.

But then...

Recently, I attended a workshop led by Scott Carley, a management development coach who helps organizations build high-performing teams. During the session, he introduced something I had never seen before: the Trust Credit Score©—a system designed to measure a leader's trustworthiness inside an organization. Like a financial credit score, it quantifies the relationship between a manager and their team. One powerful question drives the entire system: Can I trust you?

As I listened, a lightbulb went off. I immediately thought back to Donna—and the promise at the heart of her leadership. I shared the story with Scott, and he asked if I would share it with you as the foreword to his new book, *Can I Trust You?*

I jumped at the opportunity.

"Trust" is a small word—just five letters and one vowel—but it carries the weight of all relationships. "Can I trust you?" is the question behind every meaningful interaction: between managers and employees, customers and companies, doctors and patients—even strangers on the street. We ask it constantly—silently, instinctively, and often without realizing it.

In this groundbreaking book, *Can I Trust You?*, Scott Carley shares a bold, practical system for answering that question.

With the Trust Credit Score©, he offers organizations a powerful way not only to evaluate trust—but to earn it.

If you're looking for a way to turn employees into raving fans and build teams that thrive on accountability, respect, and performance, don't just read this book—study it, share it, and apply it.It's worth it.

You are worth it.

~Ralph

Ralph Peterson is a leadership expert, best-selling author, and management development coach with over 20 years of experience in long-term care. As the founder of Ralph Peterson Management Services, he helps senior care organizations empower leaders to rise to the challenge of management—especially at a time when no one wants to work.

PART I

The Foundation
of Trust

CHAPTER 1

An Executive Summary

Every day in business, whether in boardrooms, sales meetings, or casual hallway conversations, people are subconsciously asking one critical question: Can I trust you? Trust shapes every decision, partnership, and opportunity.

- Leaders ask it when delegating crucial responsibilities.
- Clients weigh it before signing contracts.
- Teams depend on it when embarking on ambitious projects.

A resounding **yes** opens doors, accelerates deals and empowers teams with clarity and confidence. When the answer is **uncertain or no**, hesitation, resistance, and slowdowns follow.

The power of trust cannot be overstated. It determines how quickly decisions are made, how effectively teams collaborate, and how much influence a leader has. A high **Trust Credit Score**™ ensures that you are seen as reliable, credible, and someone worth following. Conversely, a low score erodes confidence, stalls cooperation, and stifles growth.

Trust is the invisible currency that either accelerates or stalls success. Trust is fundamental to every relationship, from internal team dynamics to external client negotiations. To quantify and strategically elevate trust within an organization, Scott Carley, aka The Change Energizer, created the **Trust Credit Score**™ **System** —a transformative framework that measures and improves trust in the same way the FICO credit score measures financial responsibility.

Much like your FICO score determines your financial credibility, your Trust Credit Score™ opens or closes doors based on how trustworthy others perceive you. A high score fast-tracks cooperation, collaboration, and opportunities, while a low score stymies growth and success. In both finance and trust, one fundamental principle applies: **you can't talk your way out of a problem that you behaved yourself into, but you can behave your way back into trust—often faster than you think** (Stephen Covey).

The Trust Credit Score™ Concept

At its core, the Trust Credit Score™ serves as a mirror to the well-known FICO credit score. The FICO score assesses an individual's financial health and their ability to manage credit and debt, opening or closing access to opportunities such as loans, mortgages, and business funding.

Similarly, the Trust Credit Score™ evaluates how individuals, teams, and organizations are perceived in terms of trustworthiness, reliability, and integrity, either facilitating or hindering career progression, sales growth, and operational efficiency.

Just as a low FICO score blocks access to high-ticket items and investment opportunities, a low Trust Credit Score™ impedes key business relationships, stifles teamwork, and creates barriers in the sales process.

Trust, much like credit, compounds over time—small actions and behaviors accumulate to create a positive or negative perception that either fosters collaboration or breeds skepticism.

I've lived this firsthand. In my twenties, I built a massive Trust Credit Score™ as a traveling evangelist—preaching across 47 states and growing deep roots of credibility in my denomination. But in a moment of failure, I watched it collapse. A personal decision crossed a boundary, and I lost the trust of my organization, my church, and my family. Rebuilding wasn't fast. It took years. But by applying the same principles you'll find in this book—through repentance, consistency, and the behavior-based rebuild of trust—I eventually found restoration. Today, I stand as living proof: trust, once lost, can be rebuilt with intention and integrity.

Trust and the Speed of Cooperation

One of the most powerful applications of the Trust Credit Score™ lies in its impact on what Scott Carley refers to as the **Speed of Cooperation.**

The higher the trust within a team or between partners, the faster decisions are made, tasks are executed, and results are achieved. High trust eradicates friction, enabling quick, seamless collaboration. Team members openly share information, delegate responsibilities with confidence, and make critical decisions without second-guessing motives or integrity.

On the flip side, low trust within an organization grinds cooperation to a halt. **Silos emerge, communication breaks down, and decisions are delayed**—all of which lead to missed deadlines, unproductive meetings, and overall inefficiency. This slowdown in teamwork has a direct financial cost, as the time wasted navigating fractured trust leads to lost revenue, increased operational expenses, and diminished output.

In sales, the Trust Credit Score™ has a similarly profound effect.

High-trust sales teams close deals faster, retain clients longer, and generate more referrals because clients feel confident in their integrity and expertise. Conversely, a salesperson with a low Trust Credit Score finds themselves constantly fighting an uphill battle to prove their worth, leading to longer sales cycles, fewer conversions, and diminished earnings.

The Financial Impact of High and Low Trust

The financial implications of trust—or the lack thereof—are staggering. High trust within a team or organization correlates with faster project completion, reduced turnover, and increased innovation. Trust removes barriers that can otherwise cost a company valuable time and resources. The speed at which trustful teams move creates a **competitive edge in the marketplace**, allowing them to outperform their competitors and deliver superior customer experiences.

In contrast, a low Trust Credit Score™ slows everything down. Decisions are postponed as leaders and teams second-guess each other's motives and capabilities. Productivity declines as energy is redirected toward managing internal tensions rather than achieving objectives. In sales, a low-trust environment leads to churn, as customers disengage and seek more reliable partners elsewhere. The **cost of low trust** becomes visible in missed revenue targets, higher operational costs, and lost opportunities. For example, a team that consistently misses deadlines due to fractured trust may lose a key client, leading to financial strain.

The **financial benefits of high trust** are clear: greater efficiency, higher employee retention, increased sales, and stronger customer loyalty. By identifying where trust is breaking down and implementing strategies to elevate the Trust Credit Score™, organizations can boost their bottom line while fostering a more positive and collaborative culture.

Courageous Conversations: Repairing Trust by Getting Back into Character

A critical component of the Trust Credit Score™ System is the role of **Courageous Conversations**. Inspired by Disney's unique approach to casting calls (hiring for every position), this concept is about identifying when someone's performance has fallen out of alignment with their role and guiding them back "into character." Just as Disney casts each team member to embody a specific role that enhances the Disney Corporation, businesses can use a similar framework to ensure team members are aligned with their values and responsibilities. When underperformance begins to erode trust, it's not just a matter of giving feedback; it's about having a courageous conversation to realign behavior with expectations and values.

In this process, leaders work with individuals who may be struggling to keep commitments, meet deadlines, or communicate transparently—key areas impacting their Trust Credit Score™. The goal of these conversations is not to criticize but to reset and guide the individual back to their "character." By framing the discussion as an opportunity to step back into their ideal role, team members are empowered to correct behaviors, address trust fractures, and renew their commitment to the team's values and objectives. This critical dialogue repairs and elevates trust, allowing for faster cooperation and collaboration moving forward.

The Courageous Conversations approach is integral to the Trust Credit Score™ System as it provides leaders with the tools to address issues directly, authentically, and constructively, restoring trust where it's been broken. When employees are given a clear path to get back in character, they are more likely to stay aligned, productive, and deeply trusted within the organization, enhancing their own Trust Credit Score™ and positively impacting the team as a whole.

(SC) That same "casting call" approach was instrumental in my personal trust rebuild—at work, in my community, and especially with my daughters. After my divorce, I had to live out the principles I had once preached. My ex-wife tried to cut off access and influence. But I stayed consistent. I showed up. I kept my word. I focused on behavior over words. Over time, the trust was rebuilt—not overnight, but piece by piece. Today, my relationship with my daughters is strong. The work paid off.

Behavior as the Key to Rebuilding Trust

A critical principle in the Trust Credit Score framework is this: **You can't talk your way out of a problem you behaved yourself into.** If your Trust Credit Score™ is low, it's not because of what you've said—it's because of what you've done, or failed to do. Promises made but not kept, inconsistencies in communication, lack of transparency, or repeated errors all contribute to trust fractures. However, there is good news: **you can behave your way back into trust**. Small, consistent actions—such as demonstrating reliability, showing transparency in decision-making, or following through on commitments—can rebuild trust, often more quickly than expected.

Scott Carley emphasizes that **trust is built and rebuilt through behavior.** Words alone won't repair a fractured relationship or team dynamic. Trust is earned back when behavior aligns with promises, and when leaders and team members take consistent steps to demonstrate their reliability and integrity. This behavioral shift not only repairs trust but also elevates the Trust Credit Score™, creating a ripple effect throughout the organization.

Identifying Areas for Improvement

The Trust Credit Score provides a practical tool for identifying where changes need to be made to elevate one's trustworthiness. By assessing five key areas—

1. **Appearance and Body Language**
   - 55% of your communication is body language

2. **Motives and intentions**
3. **Core values and integrity**
4. **Skillset**
5. **Track record**

Individuals and organizations can pinpoint specific behaviors or actions that are eroding trust. Each of these areas offers opportunities to improve and strengthen the trust others have in you.

For instance, if an individual's Trust Credit Score™ is low in the area of **motives and intentions**, it might indicate that they're perceived as having hidden agendas or unclear objectives. In this case, focusing on transparent communication and ensuring that actions match words will help to restore trust. Similarly, a low score in **track record and results** might reflect inconsistent performance, which can be addressed by setting clear, measurable goals and delivering on promises.

Conclusion

The Trust Credit Score™ is a powerful framework that allows individuals and organizations to quantify, assess, and improve trust in meaningful, measurable ways. Created by Scott Carley, aka The Change Energizer, the Trust Credit Score™ mirrors the FICO score concept by demonstrating how trust opens or closes doors, impacting everything from internal team dynamics to external client relationships. High trust leads to faster cooperation and increased financial performance, while low trust creates friction, delays, and financial loss.

By understanding where trust is breaking down and taking actionable steps to rebuild it, individuals and teams can not only repair their Trust Credit Score™ but also elevate their performance, productivity, and profitability.

CHAPTER 2

TRUST

Your Ultimate X-Factor

Trust isn't just part of the game. **It is the game.**

When deals are big, stakes are high, and people are weighing their options, they're asking one fundamental question—even if they never say it out loud:

"Can I trust you?"

Before they open the vault, sign the deal, or bring you behind the curtain, they're running that question in the background. And they're not just looking at your resume or your pitch. They're scanning your *vibe,* your *consistency,* your *credibility,* and your *receipts.*

That's what makes **The Trust Credit Score**™ your **ultimate X-Factor.** It gives you a framework to *measure*, *track*, and *improve* the one thing that drives every decision in business and leadership: **trust.**

Why Trust is the Real Deciding Factor

It's easy to think people say yes because you have the best product, the sharpest skills, or the perfect solution. But let's be honest—**you're probably not the only one in the running.**

The person who wins the deal, lands the promotion, or gets the referral is usually the one who scores highest in trust. That includes both the *obvious* trust signals (like showing up on time and delivering results) and the *subliminal* ones (like how your energy makes people feel when you're in the room).

Trust is what people buy before they buy *anything else.*

They may not verbalize it, but they're vetting you on two levels:

The Obvious Vetting:

- Do you follow through?
- Do you show up prepared?
- Do you have the experience?
- Are you consistent?

The Subliminal Vetting:

- Do I feel safe giving you access?
- Can I trust your motives?

- Will you make me look good—or burn me?
- Do you give off integrity, or just say the right words?

If the answer to those questions is yes—*you win*. If it's no— even slightly—*you're out*.

The Trust Credit Score™: Language for What We Already Know Is Happening

Here's the problem: most people don't have the language to talk about trust clearly. They'll say, "Something just felt off," or "I'm not sure I can count on them," but they won't be able to explain *why*. That's where misunderstandings grow and missed opportunities stack up.

The Trust Credit Score™ solves that.

It gives you a shared language, a scoreboard, and a real-time feedback loop that turns vague feelings into something clear and actionable. You can *see* where trust is strong, *spot* where it's fragile, and *know* how to rebuild it.

And once you have that lens, you'll move through business and relationships with **100x more clarity and confidence** than those who are still guessing.

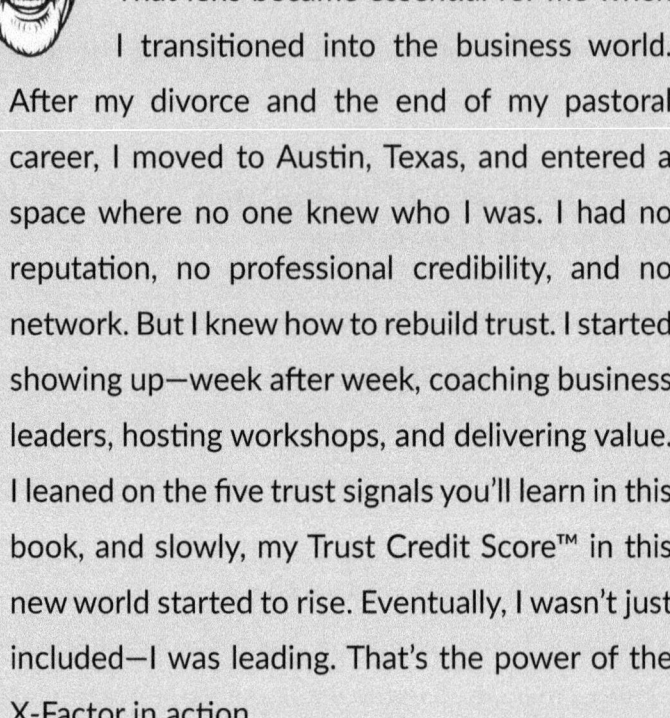

That lens became essential for me when I transitioned into the business world. After my divorce and the end of my pastoral career, I moved to Austin, Texas, and entered a space where no one knew who I was. I had no reputation, no professional credibility, and no network. But I knew how to rebuild trust. I started showing up—week after week, coaching business leaders, hosting workshops, and delivering value. I leaned on the five trust signals you'll learn in this book, and slowly, my Trust Credit Score™ in this new world started to rise. Eventually, I wasn't just included—I was leading. That's the power of the X-Factor in action.

The Speed of High-Trust Moves

In business, **speed is leverage.**

And nothing speeds things up like trust.

When trust is high:

- People say yes faster.
- Teams align with less friction.
- Clients stay longer and refer more.

- Meetings are shorter, but more productive.
- You spend less time proving yourself and more time performing.

When trust is shaky:

- Every decision feels heavy.
- People ghost you.
- Deadlines slip.
- You're constantly defending yourself, explaining yourself, and trying to recover lost ground.

The fastest way to accelerate anything in your career or business is to **build trust faster and keep it stronger.** That's what the Trust Credit Score™ equips you to do.

Five Trust Signals That Shape Every Decision

We'll go deeper into these in later chapters, but here's a snapshot of the five core trust signals to look for in yourself and others:

1. **Body Language** – Is their vibe on point, or are they giving off nervous, closed, or sketchy energy?
2. **Motives** – Are they straight-up solid, or do they feel like they're playing an angle?
3. **Values** – Are we aligned in the way we think, lead, and live?
4. **Skillset** – Are they even built for this? Do they have the chops to pull it off?

5. **Track Record** – Do they have receipts? What's their pattern of performance?

Once you can recognize these five markers, you'll have a sixth sense for trust that most people never develop.

> For me, rebuilding my track record started with the smallest wins. It meant being early to every meeting, remembering names, sending thank-you notes, and delivering real results with every client. When people didn't know my story, they judged me solely on my behavior—and that was the opportunity. When your trust signals are aligned, people begin to trust you without even realizing why. That's when momentum kicks in.

This Isn't a Personality Test—It's a Playbook

The Trust Credit Score™ isn't about labeling people. It's not a pass/fail test. It's a *tool* to help you understand where trust is being built, where it's being fractured, and what to do about it.

In fact, here's what changes when you operate with a TCS mindset:

- You ask better questions in interviews and deals.
- You navigate team dynamics with more awareness.

- You catch issues earlier—before they blow up.
- You create a culture where trust is trackable, fixable, and celebrated.

That's next-level leadership. And that's why TCS is your X-Factor.

A Trust Score Isn't Optional—You Already Have One

Here's the kicker: whether you know it or not, **people are already scoring you.**

Your team. Your clients. Your boss. Your prospects.

They're constantly watching your actions and forming a score in their minds:

Can I trust you? How much? With what?

Your choice isn't whether you *have* a Trust Credit Score—it's whether you want to *own* it and improve it.

> Rebuilding mine from the ground up taught me one truth I never forgot: Trust is the one thing you can't buy, but you can earn. And once you've earned it—especially after losing it—it becomes your most valuable asset.

The Trust Credit Score™ system isn't just a concept.

It's a competitive advantage.

It's a leadership edge.

And it's your *ultimate* X-Factor in a world that moves fast and judges quietly.

Ready to level it up?

CHAPTER 3

Trust on Credit

Trust Isn't Free – It's a Loan

How Your Actions Earn the Score That Matters

Trust operates like credit. People don't hand it over automatically—they loan it to you, often in small amounts at first, to see if you can handle it. And just like financial credit, how you "pay it back" is what determines whether that trust grows or disappears. Every interaction, promise, or decision you make is a chance to either raise your *Trust Credit Score* or watch it drop.

Why use the term *credit*? Because it perfectly captures the transactional and dynamic nature of trust. Trust isn't a static quality that exists regardless of what you do—it's constantly influenced by your actions. When you're consistent, dependable, and transparent, you're essentially making "on-time payments" that build your score. But when you break promises or act dishonestly, it's like defaulting on a loan, causing people to pull back their trust and hesitate before extending it again.

As Stephen Covey said, *"You can't talk your way out of a problem you have behaved yourself into. But you can behave yourself back into trust, and often faster than you think."*

That's the beauty of trust as credit: your actions always have the power to rebuild what's been lost. In this chapter, we'll explore why trust works like credit and how you can use that understanding to grow your score, repair fractured trust, and accelerate the Speed of Cooperation.

The Credit in Trust Score

Your *Trust Credit Score*™ mirrors your financial credit score in several key ways, making it a powerful framework for understanding how trust works in relationships and at work. Let's break it down:

1. **Trust is Loaned, Not Given Freely**
   - Just like financial credit, trust is extended with the expectation that the recipient will act responsibly. People don't automatically trust you—they wait to see if your actions

match your words. If you're new to a situation, trust starts small and builds as you prove yourself.

2. Behavior is the Currency of Trust

- Paying your bills on time builds financial credit. Similarly, consistent and reliable behavior builds your *Trust Credit Score*. It's not about what you *say*—it's what you *do* that counts.

3. Missed Payments = Fractured Trust

- Break a promise, miss a deadline, or fail to meet expectations, and it's like missing a payment on a loan. That fracture makes people question your reliability and lowers your score. Covey's insight is key here: while words may help you apologize, only your actions can truly repair the damage. Positive, consistent behavior is the currency that rebuilds trust faster than you might expect.

4. Small, Prompt Payments Build Trust

- Making small commitments and delivering on them consistently is like paying off small loans on time—it's the foundation of a strong score. Even minor actions, like showing up on time or following through on a task, send a clear message: "I'm someone you can count on."

5. Large Trust 'Loans' May Require Co-Signers

- When you're new to a role or relationship, people might need a "co-signer" to vouch for your credibility. This could be a mentor, referral, or someone who stakes their reputation on your trustworthiness until you've proven yourself.

6. **High Trust Scores Earn Better Opportunities**

- A high financial credit score unlocks better terms, and trust works the same way. When people trust you, they're more likely to promote you, collaborate with you, or give you leadership responsibilities. It's not just about being liked—it's about being seen as dependable.

Why Trust is Earned in Drops and Lost in Buckets

Building trust takes time because it's rooted in consistent, visible actions. Every time you follow through on a promise or help someone out, you're adding drops to your trust bucket. It may feel slow, but that's the nature of trust—it builds one action at a time.

However, trust can be lost in an instant. One broken promise, one moment of dishonesty, and the bucket spills, undoing weeks, months, or even years of effort. That's why trust is so fragile—it takes so long to build but so little to break.

The good news? You can refill that bucket, often faster than you think, by leaning into Covey's wisdom: *"Behave your way back into trust."* With deliberate, consistent actions, you can rebuild what's been lost and even strengthen the relationship in the process.

How to Be Proactive About Trust (And Make Your Receipts Count)

Trust isn't something you sit back and hope to earn—it's something you actively create by giving people "receipts" for your reliability. Here's how to be intentional about showing others why you're worthy of their trust.

At Work: Be the Trust MVP

1. **Volunteer for Visibility**
- Step up for projects where you can showcase your skills and reliability. Whether it's leading a team meeting or tackling a high-stakes task, find ways to put your abilities on display.
- **Why it works:** People trust what they see. Consistently delivering results shows you're someone who follows through.

2. **Solve Problems Before They're Problems**
- Don't wait to be asked—if you see an issue brewing, step in with a solution. This proactive approach signals that you're invested in the success of the team, not just your own goals.
- **Why it works:** Anticipating needs and solving problems shows leadership and dependability.

3. **Be Transparent, Even When It's Hard**
- If you hit a snag, own it. Let people know what's happening and how you're fixing it. Transparency builds trust by showing accountability.
- **Why it works:** People respect honesty and appreciate when you take responsibility instead of shifting blame.

4. **Support Your Team**

- Trust isn't just about what you do individually—it's about how you show up for others. Helping a colleague meet a deadline or sharing resources builds relational trust.
- **Why it works:** Investing in others makes them more likely to trust and rely on you.

In Personal Relationships: Build Trust One Moment at a Time

1. **Keep Your Small Promises**
- Don't underestimate the power of small actions. Whether it's showing up on time or remembering a birthday, these moments create a pattern of reliability.
- **Why it works:** Small, consistent wins build a solid foundation for trust.

2. **Be There When It Counts**
- When someone is struggling, show up fully. Offer your time, energy, or support without expecting anything in return.
- **Why it works:** People remember who was there for them when it mattered most.

3. **Own Your Mistakes**
- Messed up? Admit it, apologize, and commit to doing better. Accountability is key to rebuilding trust after a fracture.
- **Why it works:** Taking responsibility proves you value the relationship enough to make things right.

4. **Be Consistently Present**

- Trust isn't about grand gestures; it's about consistently showing up. Make it a habit to check in, follow through, and be reliable.
- **Why it works:** Consistency over time builds trust that lasts.

Why Credit Captures the Essence of Trust

Credit isn't just a financial term—it's a mindset. It's about accountability, reliability, and the constant exchange of actions that build or break confidence in someone. Trust operates the same way. Using the metaphor of credit helps us see trust as measurable, actionable, and something we can influence.

Like financial credit, trust can be repaired, rebuilt, and even optimized. The higher your *Trust Credit Score,* the more opportunities you unlock. People move faster, collaborate more easily, and invest in you when they trust you. At the end of the day, trust isn't free—it's a loan your behavior must repay.

Action Plan: Raise Your Trust Credit Score

1. **Audit Your Trust Balance**: Think about the trust "loans" you've received. Are you paying them back with consistent, reliable actions?
2. **Make Small, Visible Payments**: Focus on fulfilling small

commitments consistently. This builds trust faster than big, infrequent gestures.

3. **Repair Defaults Quickly**: If you've fractured trust, start behaving your way back with intentional, visible actions that prove your reliability.

Trust is your ultimate currency, and your behavior is the only way to earn it. Whether you're building, repairing, or accelerating trust, remember: trust is always on credit, and every action you take either raises or lowers your score.

PART II

The Five Scores of Trust

The First Score

Their Vibe is On Point

Appearance and Body Language – The First Signal of Trust

First Impressions: Your Trust Accelerator

You've heard it a million times: *You never get a second chance to make a first impression.* It's a cliché because it's true. Within seconds of meeting someone, they're subconsciously asking themselves: *Can I trust this person? Are they reliable? Are they prepared?*

Here's the wild part: **55% of communication is nonverbal.** Your appearance, posture, and gestures are doing most of the talking before you even open your mouth. And trust? It's built—or lost—right there in that split second.

But let's connect the dots: This book isn't just about making a great impression—it's about increasing the **Speed of Cooperation**. When your appearance communicates trustworthiness and confidence, people are quicker to align with you, work with you, and make decisions alongside you. Conversely, if your appearance raises red flags, it slows everything down—questions arise, hesitations creep in, and collaboration takes a backseat.

Trust, Appearance, and the Speed of Cooperation

When you show up looking polished, confident, and authentic, you send a message: *I'm here, I'm ready, and I've got this.* That message immediately sets the tone for faster collaboration and smoother interactions. Trust accelerates the Speed of Cooperation because people feel confident working with someone who looks and acts the part.

But when your appearance doesn't match the moment—think slouched posture, wrinkled clothes, or a disengaged vibe—you unintentionally throw up roadblocks. Instead of moving forward, people pause to second-guess.

The Trust Credit Score™ in Action:

Your Trust Credit Score™ is directly influenced by how you show up. A polished appearance and confident body language can give your score an immediate boost, encouraging others to work with you faster and more effectively. It's not about being perfect; it's about being intentional.

1. Confident Posture: Stand Tall, Move Fast

Your posture is your nonverbal mic drop. It tells people, *I'm here, I'm capable, and I'm ready to deliver.*

How It Speeds Up Cooperation:

- A confident stance reassures others that you're competent and engaged, reducing the need for extra explanations or reassurances.
- Good posture projects reliability, making people more willing to trust you quickly.

What Works:

- Stand tall with your shoulders back and chin up.
- Maintain a balanced stance that shows you're grounded and ready.

What Doesn't:

- Slouching or fidgeting signals insecurity or a lack of focus, slowing down trust-building.

Trust Accelerator:

- Practice a superhero pose for two minutes before a big meeting. It may sound silly, but it activates confidence in your body—and others will feel it.

2. Consistent Eye Contact: Trust at First Glance

Eye contact is like a direct line to trust. It shows you're present, honest, and genuinely interested in what's happening.

How It Speeds Up Cooperation:

- Steady eye contact helps people feel seen and valued, creating a sense of connection that accelerates collaboration.
- It eliminates doubt and builds rapport quickly.

What Works:

- Maintain natural, steady eye contact about 60–70% of the time.
- Use occasional glances away to avoid making the interaction feel too intense.

What Doesn't:

- Avoiding eye contact signals distraction or discomfort, making others hesitant to engage.

Trust Accelerator:

- If direct eye contact feels awkward, focus on the space between someone's eyes—it feels the same to them but is easier for you.

3. Genuine Smile: Trust's Fast Pass

Smiling is one of the easiest ways to break the ice and create a positive atmosphere.

How It Speeds Up Cooperation:

- A genuine smile disarms initial skepticism and sets a welcoming tone, making it easier for people to engage with you.
- Smiling is contagious—when you smile, others are more likely to mirror it, creating immediate rapport.

What Works:

- Smile naturally, letting it reach your eyes for authenticity (*hello, smizing*).
- Match your smile to the tone of the moment—warm for introductions, professional for serious discussions.

What Doesn't:

- Forced or insincere smiles come across as fake, creating mistrust instead of connection.

Trust Accelerator:

- Think of a moment that genuinely made you happy before stepping into a room—it'll make your smile feel real and inviting.

4. Clean, Professional Attire: Dress for Trust

Your clothes do more than cover you—they communicate who you are and how you want to be perceived.

How It Speeds Up Cooperation:

- A polished, intentional outfit signals readiness and respect, encouraging faster collaboration.
- Dressing appropriately for the occasion removes distractions and keeps the focus on what matters.

What Works:

- Clean, tailored clothes that fit well and suit the context.
- Adding small touches of personality, like a bold accessory or unique pattern, to stand out.

What Doesn't:

- Wrinkled, unkempt, or overly casual attire shows a lack of care, slowing down trust-building.

Trust Accelerator:

- Invest in versatile wardrobe staples—a blazer, crisp shirt, or polished shoes—that work for various professional settings.

5. Open Gestures: Speak Without Words

How you move your hands and body during conversations can make or break the vibe.

How It Speeds Up Cooperation:

- Open gestures signal transparency and approachability, encouraging others to align with you quickly.

- Relaxed movements make you seem calm and confident, reducing hesitation in others.

What Works:

- Keep your hands visible and use them to emphasize key points naturally.
- Maintain open, relaxed shoulders to project ease and confidence.

What Doesn't:

- Hiding your hands or crossing your arms signals defensiveness or discomfort.

Trust Accelerator:

- Record yourself in a mock presentation to identify any nervous or closed-off gestures, then refine them to be more open and natural.

"I Need to Be Myself": Authenticity in Appearance

Let's address the elephant in the room: *Do I really have to change how I look? Won't that make me a fraud?*

You're right to ask this. Authenticity is a cornerstone of trust. If you're not being true to yourself, people will sense it, and any trust you build will be on shaky ground.

Here's the thing: being intentional about your appearance isn't about being fake—it's about showing up as the **best version**

of yourself. Think of it like this: you wouldn't wear pajamas to a wedding, not because you're pretending to be someone else, but because you respect the occasion and want to honor it with your effort.

How to Be Authentic AND Polished

1. **Stay True to Your Style:** Your wardrobe should reflect who you are, not who you think people want you to be. Love bold colors? Rock them. Prefer minimalist looks? Own it.

2. **Speak Your Truth Through Your Vibe:** Your body language—your smile, posture, and gestures—should feel natural, not rehearsed.

3. **Balance Individuality with Professionalism:** Add touches of your personality to a polished foundation. A funky tie or statement necklace can make you memorable without overshadowing the moment.

Final Thought: Appearance Is the Gateway to Speed

Appearance isn't just about looking good—it's about building trust quickly and effectively. When you combine authenticity with intentionality, you're not only making a great first impression but also accelerating the **Speed of Cooperation.**

So, ask yourself: *What is my appearance saying about me?* When you align your look with your best self and the moment's needs, you're setting the stage for trust to flourish and collaboration to thrive.

The Speed of Cooperation

*When **trust is high**, things move faster and start clicking forward.*

Projects Actually Get Done (Fast)

1. Teams jump from idea to execution without bottlenecks, second-guessing, or waiting on a million approvals.

Collaboration Stops Feeling Like Tug-of-War

2. Silos come down. People share info, resources, and wins — no ego, just forward motion.

Innovation Doesn't Get Stuck in Draft Mode

3. Safe teams pitch bold ideas. No fear of being shut down or side-eyed. More creativity, less hesitation.

Everyone Steps Up Without Being Micromanaged

4. Trust fuels accountability. People deliver because they care, not because someone's breathing down their neck.

Crisis Mode? Teams Pivot Without the Drama

5. When things go sideways, high-trust teams don't panic — they adapt fast and figure it out together.

Scott@ScottCarley.com ✉
512-470-0570 ☎
TrustEnergizer.com 🌐

Your Trust Credit Score™

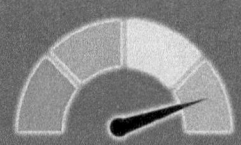

How GOOD Is It (1-10)

7

Their Vibe is On Point - Body Language

1 Confident Posture / Consistent Eye Contact / Genuine Smile / Clean and Professional Attire / Open Gestures

9

They Are Straight-Up Solid - Motives

2 Clear Intentions / Aligned Goals / Transparency / Consistency / Straightforward Communication

9

We're On The Same Page - Values

3 Keeps their Word / Shared Vibe and Values / Walks Their Talk / Owns Mistakes / Respect and Fairness

9

They Are Built For This - Skillset

4 Proven Expertise / Industry Certifications / Curiosity with Problem Solving Skills / Continuous Learning / Strong Recommendations

9

They've Got Receipts - Track Record

5 Consistent Success / Positive Outcomes / Long Term Reliability / Reputation for Excellence / Awards / Proven Impact

43 / 5 = **8.6**

Scott@ScottCarley.com ✉
TrustEnergizer.com 🌐
512-470-0570 📞

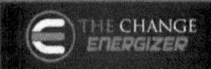 THE CHANGE ENERGIZER

CHAPTER 5

The Second Score

They Are Straight Up Solid

Motives and Intentions – The Second Signal of Trust

What's Your Deal? Why Motives Matter

L et's cut to the chase: people want to know *why* you're here. Are you genuinely invested in the team, the mission, and the company—or are you just looking out for yourself? Your motives and intentions are like the invisible current that drives every interaction. If people sense your hearts in the right place, they're all in. But if your vibe is even slightly off, trust will nosedive faster than a bad stock tip, and with it, so will the **Speed of Cooperation.**

Motives are what separate *partners* from *players*. They're not just about what you want but about how aligned you are with the bigger picture. If you can show people that you're here to help them win—and you actually mean it—you're not only building trust but accelerating how quickly and seamlessly people will work with you.

Trust and the Speed of Cooperation

When motives are clear and aligned with the company's vision, trust flows freely, and that trust fuels the **Speed of Cooperation.** Think about it: when you trust someone's intentions, you don't waste time questioning their agenda or double-checking their work. Teams move faster, decisions are made with confidence, and everyone operates in sync.

But the reverse is also true. When trust in motives breaks down, cooperation slows to a crawl. Meetings get longer because no one feels comfortable taking action without layers of approval. Misunderstandings pile up, and instead of working together, people start working around each other. The cost? Missed deadlines, wasted energy, and a culture of doubt.

The Trust Litmus Test: Are You in It for the Vision?

Here's the thing: companies, teams, and even individual clients are constantly scanning for one key thing: *Are you here for the long haul, or are you just here for you?*

When your motives align with the company's vision or the client's goals, people feel safe trusting you. That trust creates a direct line to cooperation—fewer obstacles, quicker decisions, and stronger collaboration.

What Genuine Support Looks Like

1. **Understanding the Bigger Picture**: You know the company's mission, values, and objectives—and you're excited about them.
2. **Contributing Beyond Your Role**: You're willing to lend a hand or offer ideas outside your specific job description because you care about the team's success.
3. **Celebrating Others' Wins**: You're just as hyped about a coworker's promotion or a team success as you would be about your own.

Real Talk: If you're only focused on how a situation benefits you, people will feel it. Support has to be *real,* not performative. Genuine support unlocks trust, and trust speeds up everything— from problem-solving to innovation.

Motives 101: The Trust Builders

1. Genuine Care: You're Actually Here for the Team

People can sense when you actually *care*—and it's magnetic. Genuine care isn't just about being nice; it's about showing up for the company's vision and your teammates, even when it's inconvenient or hard.

How It Increases the Speed of Cooperation:

- When people believe you're invested in their success, they respond by aligning with you. No second-guessing, no foot-dragging—just seamless collaboration.

What Works:

- Actively listening to others' ideas and concerns.
- Offering help, even when it's not part of your job.
- Showing enthusiasm for the company's mission and how you fit into it.

What Doesn't:

- Fake niceness—people can spot a "team player" who's only looking out for themselves.
- Helping only when it benefits you directly.

Trust Accelerator:

- Ask yourself: *How can I contribute to this vision?* Look for opportunities to make an impact, even in small ways, that show you're genuinely invested.

2. Transparency: Keep It Real

Transparency is about putting your cards on the table. Whether you're pitching an idea, handling a mistake, or discussing goals, being honest about your intentions builds trust faster than any grand gesture.

How It Increases the Speed of Cooperation:

- When people don't have to decode your motives, they can focus on moving forward. Transparency eliminates the friction caused by doubt or second-guessing.

What Works:

- Being upfront about your goals and aligning them with the team's goals.
- Admitting when you don't know something or when you've messed up.

What Doesn't:

- Hidden agendas, vague promises, or sugarcoating bad news.
- Saying what you think people want to hear instead of what's true.

Trust Accelerator:

- Practice saying what you mean in a way that's clear and respectful. For example: *"I'm really excited about this opportunity because I believe it aligns with our long-term goals."*

3. Aligned Goals: You're Rowing the Same Boat

Trust skyrockets when people see you're not just chasing your own agenda—you're aligned with their goals and the company's vision.

How It Increases the Speed of Cooperation:

- When everyone's rowing in the same direction, there's no need for constant course corrections. Alignment creates momentum and cuts down on wasted effort.

What Works:

- Framing your work as part of the bigger picture: *"This project is important because it helps us hit the team's quarterly target."*
- Asking questions to understand how your role supports the larger mission.

What Doesn't:

- Pursuing personal goals that conflict with the team's priorities.
- Failing to connect your work to the company's vision.

Trust Accelerator:

- During team meetings or one-on-ones, explicitly tie your ideas or updates to broader company objectives. This shows you're thinking big-picture, not just "me-picture."

Real-Life Story: The Aligned Vision Win

Imagine this: You're working on a big marketing campaign, and your boss is focused on hitting quarterly revenue goals. Instead of just completing your tasks, you approach your boss and say, *"I noticed this campaign ties directly to our Q4 revenue goals. What else can I do to help us maximize results?"*

Boom. You've just shown you're not just there to check boxes— you're aligned with the bigger picture. That level of genuine investment turns heads, builds trust, and accelerates cooperation. Now, instead of micromanaging you, your boss is trusting you to take initiative, and the team moves faster as a result.

Final Thought: Lead with Purpose

Motives and intentions are the hidden drivers of trust. When your actions consistently align with the company's vision, when you're transparent about your goals, and when you genuinely care about the team's success, trust isn't just earned—it's supercharged.

And that trust? It's the key to unlocking the **Speed of Cooperation**. With trust in your motives, people will work with you—not against you. Decisions will come faster, teamwork will feel effortless, and the company's vision will transform from a lofty goal into a shared reality.

So ask yourself: *Am I here for the mission, or just for me?* When you show up for the mission with genuine support, people notice. And trust? It follows naturally — bringing the Speed of Cooperation with it.

CHAPTER 6

The Third Score

We're On The Same Page

Integrity—The Third Signal of Trust

Walk the Talk: The Heart of Integrity

Integrity is the real MVP of trust. It's not just about what you say; it's about what you do. Do your actions back up your words? Do you actually deliver on your promises? If the answer is yes, you're stacking trust points with every interaction. If the answer is no, you're in trust debt—and believe me, that's a tough hole to climb out of.

At its core, integrity is about alignment: your words, actions,

core values, and promises working in sync. It's about being the same person in every room—whether it's with your boss, your team, or your clients. When people see that your integrity is rock solid, trust spreads like wildfire—and that trust is the engine that drives the Speed of Cooperation, a key theme of this book.

Trust, Integrity, Core Values, and the Speed of Cooperation

Think of integrity and core values as trust accelerators. Core values serve as the compass for your decisions and actions. When your behavior consistently reflects your values, people know they can count on you. This eliminates bottlenecks and speeds up everything: decision-making, teamwork, and execution.

But here's the flip side: when integrity or core values are compromised, everything slows down. People start double-checking your work, questioning your motives, and creating backup plans. Trust erodes, and with it, the Speed of Cooperation.

The Trust Credit Score™ in Action

Your Trust Credit Score™ is like a dashboard for measuring the health of your integrity and core values. The higher your score, the faster people will work with you because they know you'll deliver with consistency and authenticity. Want to raise the Speed of Cooperation on your team? Start by aligning your actions with your core values and making sure your behavior consistently matches your words.

The Trust Triangle: Alignment, Authenticity, Core Values, and Delivering on Promises

When people think about integrity, they often imagine big, dramatic moments of heroism. But trust isn't built in the big moments—it's built in the small, consistent ones. Here's how integrity and core values break down into four core elements:

1. Alignment: Does Your Behavior Match Your Words?

Integrity starts with being congruent—fancy word, but it means your words, actions, and values match up. It's about living your values, not just talking about them.

Why It Builds Trust and Speeds Cooperation:

- When your behavior aligns with what you say, people know they don't have to micromanage you. Decisions happen faster, and the team moves forward with confidence.
- Alignment eliminates second-guessing and builds momentum.

Why It Fails:

- Saying one thing and doing another is the fastest way to tank trust. It screams, *I'm not who I say I am.*
- Misalignment slows cooperation because people start questioning your every move.

Trust Accelerator:

- Audit yourself. Are you consistently acting in ways that reflect your core values and promises? If not, fix it—fast.

Ask yourself: *If my Trust Credit Score was public, would people believe it's accurate?*

2. Core Values: Are They Guiding Your Decisions?

Your core values are your true north—the principles that guide your decisions and actions. Living by them builds trust and speeds cooperation because they reflect what you stand for.

Why It Builds Trust and Speeds Cooperation:

- When your decisions consistently reflect your core values, people know what to expect and can rely on you.
- Core values help resolve conflicts faster because they provide a clear standard for decision-making.

Why It Fails:

- Ignoring or compromising your values creates confusion and mistrust.
- People will hesitate to trust you if your actions don't reflect the values you claim to have.

Trust Accelerator:

- Identify your top five core values and check how well your daily actions align with them. If there's a gap, bridge it.

3. Authenticity: Are You the Real Deal?

Authenticity isn't about being perfect—it's about being

real. It's owning your strengths, acknowledging your flaws, and showing up as your true self.

Why It Builds Trust and Speeds Cooperation:

- Authenticity creates clarity. When people know who you really are, they don't have to waste time decoding your intentions.
- Being real about your capabilities makes collaboration easier because people know exactly what to expect from you.

Why It Fails:

- Phoniness is a trust killer. If people feel like you're wearing a mask, they'll question everything you say.
- Pretending to know more than you do can lead to costly mistakes and slower problem-solving.

Trust Accelerator:

- Be yourself, but be your best self. Share your wins and your lessons learned—people trust those who embrace both.

4. Delivering on Promises: Do You Follow Through?

Every promise you make is a check against your integrity. Fulfilling that promise is how you keep your Trust Credit Score™ in the black.

Why It Builds Trust and Speeds Cooperation:

- Following through proves you're reliable. It eliminates

unnecessary follow-ups and keeps the team moving at full speed.

- Consistent delivery builds trust, leading to smoother communication and faster results.

Why It Fails:

- Breaking promises creates trust debt, and it's hard to dig out of that hole.
- Missed commitments slow cooperation because people start hesitating to depend on you.

Trust Accelerator:

- Be realistic about your commitments. Under-promise and over-deliver whenever possible. If something changes, communicate early and clearly.

Integrity in Action: From Slow to Go

Picture this: Your team is launching a new product, and the timeline is tight. You've got two teammates.

- **Teammate A** always delivers on time, communicates openly about challenges, and admits when they need help.
- **Teammate B** overpromises, hides mistakes, and sometimes ghosts on follow-ups.

Who do you trust to help hit the deadline? Teammate A, no question. Their integrity and alignment with core values raise the Speed of Cooperation. Meanwhile, Teammate B slows everything down by creating doubt and extra work for everyone else.

Lesson: Be Teammate A. Every single time.

Using Integrity and Core Values to Boost Your Trust Credit Score™

Want to raise your Trust Credit Score™ and turbocharge the Speed of Cooperation? Focus on integrity and core values. Here's how:

1. **Be Predictable:** Consistency is key. When people know what to expect from you, they'll trust you faster.
2. **Own Your Mistakes:** Messed up? Admit it. Taking responsibility shows maturity and commitment to fixing things.
3. **Communicate Early and Often:** Keep people in the loop. Surprises might be fun for birthdays, but not for deadlines.

Final Thought: Integrity and Core Values Are Your Superpowers

Integrity and core values aren't just nice-to-haves—they're game-changers. When your behavior aligns with your words, when you live your core values, and when you consistently deliver on your promises, you're not just building trust—you're building momentum.

And that momentum? It fuels the Speed of Cooperation, creating a ripple effect that drives faster decisions, smoother teamwork, and bigger wins for everyone involved.

So ask yourself: *Is my integrity raising my Trust Credit Score™?* Because when integrity and core values are your foundation, trust becomes your legacy—and cooperation moves at the speed of trust.

CHAPTER 7

The Fourth Score

They Are Built For This

Expertise and Skillset–The Fourth Signal of Trust

Are They Built for This?

When it comes to trust, nothing screams *reliable* like knowing someone has the skills to back it up. Whether it's a surgeon performing a complex operation, a designer creating your brand's logo, or a teammate leading a major project, their ability to deliver comes down to one question: *Are they built for this?*

Your **skillset** isn't just what you *know*—it's what you can *show*. It's the hard evidence that you have what it takes to solve problems, make an impact, and consistently deliver results. And in the world of The Trust Credit Score™, your skillset plays a starring role in how quickly people decide to trust you.

Skillset and the Speed of Cooperation

Let's connect the dots: when someone believes in your skills, they stop overthinking and start trusting. They're more likely to delegate, collaborate, and greenlight decisions without hesitation. That's the magic of a strong skillset—it doesn't just build trust; it fuels the **Speed of Cooperation.**

But what happens when people doubt your skills? Cooperation slows to a crawl. Meetings get longer because everyone wants to double-check the plan. Projects hit roadblocks because no one is sure you can pull it off. Trust in your skillset is the difference between momentum and stagnation.

The Trust Credit Score™ in Action:

Your skillset directly impacts your Trust Credit Score™. A strong score signals that you're not just equipped—you're *proven*. And the higher your score, the faster people will work with you because they know you've got the tools to make things happen.

The Five Elements of a Trustworthy Skillset

1. Proven Expertise: You've Got the Receipts

Expertise isn't just about knowing stuff—it's about knowing the *right* stuff and applying it effectively. It's what makes people think, *They've been here before—they know what they're doing.*

How It Boosts the Speed of Cooperation:

- Proven expertise eliminates doubt. People trust your recommendations and decisions without feeling the need to micromanage.
- Teams move faster because they don't have to spend time second-guessing your abilities.

What Works:

- Specializing in an area where you consistently deliver results.
- Staying updated on industry trends and best practices to keep your knowledge sharp.

What Doesn't:

- Bluffing expertise when you're out of your depth—it's a fast track to losing trust.

Trust Accelerator:

- Regularly invest in learning. Take courses, attend workshops, and read widely. Expertise isn't static—it evolves, and so should you.

2. Industry Certifications: Trust Badges That Speak for Themselves

Certifications are like gold stars for grown-ups. They show that you've done the work, passed the tests, and have the chops to deliver.

How It Boosts the Speed of Cooperation:

- Certifications act as a trust shortcut. They give people confidence in your abilities without needing a trial run.
- Teams and clients are more likely to give you responsibility upfront because your credentials do the talking.

What Works:

- Highlighting certifications that directly relate to your role or goals.
- Using certifications as a conversation starter to showcase your expertise.

What Doesn't:

- Overloading your résumé with outdated or irrelevant certifications.

212° Trust Accelerator

- Focus on quality over quantity. A few well-chosen certifications carry more weight than a laundry list of unrelated credentials.

3. Problem-Solving Skills: You're the Fixer

Skills aren't just about knowledge—they're about application. Problem-solving is where you take what you know and turn it into solutions that work.

How It Boosts the Speed of Cooperation:

- People don't hesitate to involve you because they know you'll find a way to get things done.
- Quick, effective solutions keep projects on track and eliminate delays caused by uncertainty.

What Works:

- Breaking down complex problems into manageable steps.
- Staying calm under pressure and focusing on actionable solutions.

What Doesn't:

- Avoiding challenges or passing the buck—it shows a lack of confidence in your skills.

212° Trust Accelerator:

- Frame challenges as opportunities to flex your expertise. The more problems you solve, the higher your Trust Credit Score™ climbs.

4. Reputation for Excellence: Let Your Work Speak for You

Your reputation is the loudest voice in the room. When others consistently vouch for your skills and results, you become the go-to person people trust.

How It Boosts the Speed of Cooperation:

- A strong reputation means people are more likely to follow your lead without hesitation.
- Referrals and endorsements can open doors faster than even the best pitch.

What Works:

- Building relationships with people who can speak to your abilities.
- Consistently delivering high-quality work that exceeds expectations.

What Doesn't:

- Letting a bad reputation linger without addressing it—it's trust kryptonite.

212° Trust Accelerator:

- Ask for testimonials or endorsements from colleagues, clients, or mentors. A glowing recommendation is a trust booster and a cooperation accelerator.

5. Awards and Proven Impact: The Cherry on Top

Awards and measurable outcomes are the ultimate trust flex.

They're proof that not only can you do the work—you're exceptional at it.

How It Boosts the Speed of Cooperation:

- Awards build instant credibility, making people more likely to trust your ideas.
- Tangible results (like revenue growth or efficiency gains) show that your skills deliver real value.

What Works:

- Showcasing results that directly tie to team or company goals.
- Sharing awards as part of a broader narrative about your impact.

What Doesn't:

- Flaunting irrelevant or exaggerated achievements—it comes off as insincere.

212° Trust Accelerator:

- Focus on impact over accolades. It's great to win awards, but measurable results carry even more weight in building trust.

Using Skillset to Level Up Your Trust Credit Score™

If you want to fast-track cooperation and skyrocket your Trust Credit Score™, your skillset is the place to start. Here's how:

1. **Identify Your Strengths:** What are you *really* good at? Focus on areas where you can consistently deliver results.

2. **Fill the Gaps:** If there's a skill you're missing, go get it. Lifelong learning isn't just a buzzword—it's your secret weapon.

3. **Show Your Work:** Don't assume people know what you're capable of. Share your successes, but frame them in terms of how they've helped others or the team.

Real-Life Story: Skillset and Speed in Action

Picture this: A project deadline is looming, and your team needs a graphics expert to quickly design a pitch deck. One team member has a killer portfolio and a track record of delivering under pressure. Another claims they can do it but has never shown proof.

Who do you trust to get the job done? The answer is obvious. The team moves faster, communicates better and meets the deadline because trust in that person's skillset speeds up every step of the process.

Final Thought: Build Your Skillset, Build Your Trust

Your skillset isn't just a box to check—it's your trust accelerator. When you combine proven expertise, relevant certifications, problem-solving superpowers, a reputation for excellence, and tangible results, you're sending a clear message: *I'm built for this.*

And when people trust your skills, the Speed of Cooperation skyrockets. Decisions happen faster, teamwork becomes seamless, and projects move from concept to completion without unnecessary roadblocks.

So, what's your skillset saying about you? Make it loud, make it clear, and make it count—because every skill you sharpen boosts your Trust Credit Score™ and accelerates your path to success.

CHAPTER 8

The Fifth Score

They've Got Receipts

Track Record–The Fifth Signal of Trust

They've Got Receipts

Trust isn't just about what you say you can do—it's about what you've *already* done. Your **track record** is the proof that you've shown up, delivered, and crushed it. It's not hypothetical; it's the cold, hard evidence that you've been there, done that, and made it happen.

While **skillset is about potential,** your **track record is about** *performance.* It's the receipts people need to believe in you without hesitation. And in the context of **The Trust Credit Score**™, a strong track record is the ultimate trust booster. It shows you're reliable, consistent, and capable, which speeds up cooperation in ways that words alone never can.

Track Record and the Speed of Cooperation

Here's the reality: when people trust your track record, they skip the doubts and delays. They don't need endless meetings to triple-check your plan or micromanage your execution—they know you'll deliver. That trust accelerates the **Speed of Cooperation**, turning drawn-out processes into streamlined successes.

But when your track record is shaky or nonexistent? It's like hitting the brakes. Doubts creep in, decisions get delayed, and cooperation slows to a crawl. A strong track record is like a fast pass—it gets you straight to trust, bypassing the usual bottlenecks.

The Trust Credit Score™ in Action:

Your track record directly impacts your Trust Credit Score™. A proven history of results raises your score and makes it easier for others to work with you quickly and confidently.

The Three Dimensions of a Track Record

1. Long-Term Track Record: Consistency Over Time

This is your legacy layer—the cumulative proof that you've been delivering the goods for years. It's the story of your reliability, painted over time.

Why It Speeds Up Cooperation:

- A long-term track record eliminates doubts about your consistency. People know you don't just get lucky— you're dependable.

- Teams and clients trust you to handle high-stakes projects because you've got a history of delivering.

How It Impacts Trust:

- A long history of wins creates trust that feels effortless. You've proven yourself, so people don't waste time questioning your ability.

212° Trust Accelerator:[1]

- Keep a running list of your major accomplishments, especially ones tied to measurable results. Whether it's revenue growth, team successes, or innovative solutions, your history is your trust currency.

2. Short-Term Track Record: Fresh Wins

Even if you don't have a decades-long history, you can build trust with recent successes. In fact, people often care more about what you've done *lately* than what you achieved years ago.

---

[1] 212° is a metaphor; At 211° water is hot. But at 212° it becomes steam that can power a locomotive. S.L. Parker

Why It Speeds Up Cooperation:

- Fresh results show you're still in the game, actively delivering value.
- Teams feel confident collaborating with you because they see you're on a winning streak.

How It Impacts Trust:

- Short-term wins build momentum, especially for new roles, industries, or relationships.
- It's proof you can adapt and succeed in today's environment, not just in the past.

212° Trust Accelerator:

- Don't underestimate the power of recent victories. Even small wins—like completing a challenging task ahead of schedule—can be framed as part of your growing track record.

3. Translating Track Record: Bringing Your Wins to New Contexts

One of the most underrated aspects of a track record is its adaptability. A great track record in one area can be translated to build trust in a completely different context—as long as you connect the dots for people.

Why It Speeds Up Cooperation:

- Translating your experience shows you're adaptable, which is a huge trust signal in new situations.
- People trust you faster when they see parallels between your past successes and the challenges at hand.

How It Impacts Trust:

- A well-translated track record builds instant credibility, even in unfamiliar roles or industries.
- It reduces hesitation and accelerates buy-in because people see how your skills transfer.

212° Trust Accelerator:

- When stepping into a new role or industry, frame your past wins in terms that resonate with the new audience. For example, if you led a successful marketing campaign, explain how those leadership skills apply to managing a team in a different field.

The Speed of Cooperation: Track Record in Action

Imagine a team is launching a product under a tight deadline. One team member has a stellar track record of managing similar projects, delivering results on time and under budget. Another has potential but no receipts to back it up.

Who does the team trust to lead the charge? It's a no-brainer. The person with the proven track record accelerates cooperation because the team knows they'll deliver. Meetings are shorter, decisions come faster, and everyone operates with confidence.

Now flip the script. If no one has a clear track record, the team spends time second-guessing, double-checking, and worrying about what might go wrong. Cooperation slows and so does progress.

Building a Stronger Track Record

If you want to raise your Trust Credit Score™ and boost the Speed of Cooperation, focus on strengthening your track record. Here's how:

1. Stack Your Wins

- Don't wait for the perfect opportunity to prove yourself—start building your track record today. Whether it's small victories or major milestones, every win adds up.

2. Document Your Impact

- Keep detailed records of your accomplishments. Numbers speak louder than words, so track things like revenue growth, efficiency gains, or project completion rates.

3. Translate Your Experience

- When moving into a new role or industry, don't assume people will connect the dots for you. Explain how your past successes are relevant to the current situation.

Real-Life Story: Translating a Track Record

Let's say you're transitioning from a corporate role into a startup environment. Your track record in managing multimillion-dollar budgets might seem irrelevant at first glance. But if you frame it as "maximizing limited resources to deliver high-impact results," suddenly it clicks. You've proven you can handle the fast-paced, resource-constrained challenges startups face.

Lesson: A great track record isn't limited by context—it's limited by your ability to explain it.

Final Thought: Your Track Record Is Your Fast Pass

Your track record is more than a résumé—it's your **trust résumé**. It's the proof that you've delivered results, solved problems, and made an impact. And when people trust your track record, they don't hesitate—they act.

That's the power of a strong track record: it fuels the **Speed of Cooperation**, making collaboration seamless, decisions faster, and success inevitable.

So ask yourself: *What do my receipts say about me?* Because every project, every success, and every lesson learned is another brick in the foundation of trust—and another step toward accelerating your Trust Credit Score™.

PART III

Applying the Trust Credit Score

CHAPTER 9

Why CEOs Want to Use the Trust Credit Score™ System

The Strategic Advantage of Trust

As a CEO, you understand that trust is not just a soft skill—it's a business multiplier. Just like financial credit scores determine borrowing power, the Trust Credit Score™ system determines the speed, efficiency, and effectiveness of your organization. In a complex, fast-moving business environment, trust is the lubricant that enables smoother operations, faster decision-making, and stronger relationships—both internally and externally.

The Business Case for Trust

Trust directly impacts critical business areas that affect operational success:

- **Productivity** – High-trust teams require fewer approvals, operate with less oversight, and execute more efficiently. When employees trust leadership and their peers, work gets done faster, with fewer roadblocks and bottlenecks.

- **Collaboration & Speed** – In high-trust environments, teams and departments communicate more openly, share resources, and solve problems collaboratively, leading to faster execution and innovation.

- **Employee Retention & Engagement** – Employees who trust their leaders and colleagues are more engaged, take greater initiative, and are less likely to leave. Reduced turnover leads to significant cost savings in hiring and training.

- **Customer & Investor Confidence** – When trust is embedded internally, it extends externally, influencing investor confidence and customer loyalty. Organizations with strong trust consistently outperform their competitors in market reputation and stakeholder satisfaction.

Why It Matters: Trust isn't just a cultural initiative—it's a strategic advantage that drives growth, profitability, and innovation.

The Dual Trust Credit Score™ System

The Trust Credit Score™ system offers a two-pronged approach—both proactive and reactive—to managing trust within an organization.

- **Trust Credit Score™ (Positive Model)** – This proactive framework assesses and strengthens trust across leadership, teams, and external partnerships. It highlights areas of strength and identifies opportunities for growth, ensuring that high-performance teams maintain trust at their core.

- **Trust Credit Score™ (Crash Model)** – A structured system for diagnosing and repairing fractured trust. Leadership missteps, internal conflicts, or customer trust issues are inevitable, but this model provides a clear roadmap for restoring confidence and preventing further damage.

By integrating both models, companies can prevent small trust fractures from escalating into full-scale breakdowns that affect productivity, team morale, and customer relationships.

How the Trust Credit Score™ Works

Trust is assessed across five critical areas that impact business operations:

- **Body Language** – Leaders set the tone through non-verbal communication. Open, confident body language fosters trust, while closed or inconsistent cues create doubt and hesitation.

- **Motives** – Transparency in leadership builds alignment and security. Employees need to trust that decisions are made with integrity and not hidden agendas.

- **Integrity** – Words must align with actions. Consistency and accountability reinforce trust, while broken commitments lead to skepticism and disengagement.

- **Skillset** – Competence in leadership and execution reassures teams and stakeholders that the organization is capable of delivering on its promises.

- **Track Record** – A history of consistent results builds trust over time. Leaders with a strong track record earn credibility, while those with a pattern of failure must work harder to regain trust.

Why It Matters: CEOs who measure and manage trust can pinpoint weaknesses in leadership, team dynamics, and customer relationships before they become larger business risks.

The Cost of Trust Breakdowns

Fractured trust carries significant costs that are often overlooked:

- **Missed Deadlines & Bottlenecks** – When teams don't trust leadership or each other, they delay decisions, second-guess instructions, and operate with inefficiencies that slow down execution.

- **Turnover & Talent Loss** – Employees disengage when they feel uncertain about leadership, leading to increased turnover, recruitment costs, and disruptions in workflow.
- **Reputation Damage** – Trust breakdowns extend beyond internal teams. Customers, investors, and partners lose confidence in organizations that display inconsistencies, leading to long-term credibility issues.

Why CEOs Should Care

Trust breakdowns are costly, affecting morale, productivity, and public perception. Addressing trust proactively prevents revenue loss, internal conflict, and brand damage.

Tangible Business Outcomes

The Trust Credit Score™ system delivers measurable improvements in key areas:

Increased Efficiency – Reducing bureaucratic red tape enables faster decision-making, allowing teams to work with autonomy and confidence.

Better Decision-Making – Open, trust-based environments foster transparency, leading to stronger collaboration and innovation at all levels.

Higher Morale & Retention – When employees trust

leadership, they are more engaged and committed, reducing turnover and recruitment costs.

- **Faster Crisis Recovery** – When trust is broken, the Crash Model provides a structured approach to resolving issues quickly and effectively, minimizing long-term damage.
- **Why It Matters:** High-trust organizations operate at peak efficiency, retain top talent, and recover from setbacks faster—giving them a competitive edge in their industries.

Implementation: Seamless & Scalable

One of the greatest advantages of the Trust Credit Score™ system is its ease of integration into existing business processes. CEOs don't need to overhaul company structures to implement this framework.

- **Performance Reviews & Leadership Development** – Use the Positive Trust Credit Score™ to measure leadership effectiveness and strengthen organizational trust over time.
- **Conflict Resolution & Crisis Management** – Apply the Crash Model when trust fractures occur, ensuring a structured approach to rebuilding relationships and maintaining productivity.
- **Cultural Integration & Growth** – Embedding trust metrics into company culture initiatives creates long-term stability and a resilient organizational structure.

Why It Works for CEOs: The system is flexible, scalable, and can be tailored to individual departments or company-wide initiatives without disrupting ongoing operations.

A CEO's Legacy: Leading with Trust

At the highest level, trust defines a CEO's legacy. Financial success is critical, but a leader's true impact is measured by the strength of the organization they leave behind. High-trust companies move faster, collaborate more effectively, and maintain stronger customer and investor relationships.

Building a trust-first culture is not just an operational necessity—it is a leadership imperative. CEOs who prioritize trust lay the foundation for long-term, sustainable success, ensuring their companies remain resilient and competitive in an ever-changing business landscape.

Final Takeaway: The Trust Credit Score™ system provides a clear, actionable framework for embedding trust into the DNA of an organization. By measuring, strengthening, and repairing trust at every level, CEOs can optimize efficiency, enhance reputation, and drive long-term profitability.

Build trust. Accelerate cooperation. Drive success.

CHAPTER 10

Using Disney's "Casting-Call" for Hiring

D isney has long referred to its **job openings** as "casting calls," drawing inspiration from its entertainment roots. This terminology ties back to the company's origins in show business, where actors and performers would audition for roles in films and theme park shows. Walt Disney himself is said to have wanted every employee to see themselves as part of a larger production, with each person playing a specific role in creating the magic of Disney.

By calling its job postings "casting calls," Disney reinforces the idea that everyone, from the performers to the corporate staff, plays a part in the overall "show" that is Disney. Employees are considered "cast members," regardless of their position, and their jobs are referred to as their "roles." This language serves to create a sense of unity and immersion, where everyone feels like they are part of the storytelling and guest experience, whether they are in front-line roles in the theme parks or working behind the scenes in corporate offices.

This approach has helped Disney maintain a strong culture that emphasizes teamwork, creativity, and customer experience, aligning all employees with the same vision of delivering a magical and cohesive experience to guests. By extending this theatrical language to white-collar positions, Disney ensures that even the business side of operations is seen as part of the creative process, maintaining the company's brand values across all levels.

Using Disney's **Casting Call** idea for hiring a Division Manager in a tech company, here's a creative framework focusing on roles, duties, teamwork, character gifting, KPIs, and reporting:

Ocean's 11 Unbelievable Team Heist

When people think of *Ocean's 11*, they usually remember the charm, the cleverness, and the cool-factor. But what makes the movie unforgettable—and worth modeling—isn't just the heist. It's how the heist worked.

Danny Ocean didn't pull off a miracle with raw charisma alone.

He built a team where every person had a defined role, a specialized strength, and a moment when the entire mission hinged on their performance. No role was filler. Every role was essential.

That's exactly how **high-trust teams function** in the real world. Rusty was operations—cool, clear, and always one step ahead. Basher's tech genius got them into spaces no one else could touch. Yen's physical agility was the literal key to breaching the vault. Saul brought institutional wisdom. Livingston managed the nerves and the surveillance. Linus was green, but gifted—and proved himself when it counted. Even Frank, who seemed minor, became critical at just the right time.

Now imagine trying to run that job with fractured trust. Imagine bringing in someone with unclear motives, questionable follow-through, or a pattern of miscommunication. It wouldn't just slow the job down—**it would jeopardize the whole thing.**

That's where **The Trust Credit Score**™ system becomes your **secret weapon** in team building.

The TCS framework gives you real insight into the behaviors that predict performance and protect alignment. Before you bring someone into a mission-critical role, you can evaluate:

- **Body Language:** Are they giving off confidence or chaos?
- **Motives:** Do they play for the team—or just themselves?
- **Values:** Are they aligned with your mission and your culture?
- **Skillset:** Do they actually have the chops to pull this off under pressure?

- **Track Record:** Have they shown up strong—and consistently—when it mattered most?

A traditional resume can't show you those things. But behavior can. And TCS helps you translate behavior into a score that drives better decisions.

Let's say you're putting together a team for a massive financial audit. Big client. Complex reporting. Tight deadlines. There's no room for guesswork. You're not just assigning based on seniority—you're casting for trust. Using TCS, you might score a potential lead at an 8 for track record, a 9 in skillset, but only a 5 in motives—maybe they've shown signs of being self-serving or withholding key info. That score would tell you: this isn't the right time to place them in a leadership role. Not yet.

On the flip side, your up-and-comer may only have a 6 on track record but is scoring 9s on values, motives, and behavior under pressure. With coaching, they may be the right pinch hitter when a deadline tightens or a client escalates.

This is what makes the Trust Credit Score™ so powerful—it's **not about judgment**, it's about clarity. It gives you a way to **build with confidence**, staff with precision, and set every person up for success.

In a high-stakes, high-impact project, you can't afford to wing it. You need a crew you trust. And you need a system to **build trust before the first move is ever made.**

That's what TCS delivers.

It's your **Danny Ocean lens** for building *unstoppable teams*.

CHAPTER 11

How to Score a Trust Crash

The Trust Credit Score (Crash): Measuring Broken Trust and Rebuilding Faster

Trust isn't just a warm, fuzzy feeling—it's currency. It determines whether deals get done, teams thrive, or relationships fall apart. And just like money, trust can be saved, spent, invested, or lost in a flash. The problem? Most people operate in a world where they either blindly trust or second-guess everyone, with no system to quantify what's really happening.

That's why being able to measure trust—objectively—is an absolute game-changer. You can't fix what you can't measure, and when trust takes a hit, knowing exactly *where* it's broken is the key to repairing it. That's the power of The Trust Credit Score (Crash) system. It provides a structured way to evaluate fractured trust and lays out a clear path to recovery.

The Power of Scoring Trust

Most people think of trust as all-or-nothing—you either have it, or you don't. But trust is more nuanced than that. Just like a credit score determines financial trustworthiness, your Trust Credit Score determines your trustworthiness in personal and professional relationships. And when trust is damaged, we need a way to diagnose the problem.

Enter the *Crash* model. Instead of just measuring strengths, this version of the Trust Credit Score focuses on where trust is *broken* and to what extent. The goal isn't just to point out issues—it's to help people understand *why* trust is fractured so they can take the right steps to rebuild it.

(SC) When I hit my own Trust Crash in 2000, I didn't need someone to just tell me I'd made a mistake. I already knew that. What I didn't know was how to identify the areas where trust had been fractured—and what to do about it. My motives had come into question. My integrity had taken a hit. And my track record, up to that point spotless, was overshadowed by a personal failure. The Trust Credit Score™ (Crash) system didn't exist then—but I lived every step of it. And I can tell you: this process matters.

How to Score the Trust Credit Score (Crash) Model

Scoring the Crash model is simple, yet powerful. It follows a step-by-step process to assess the five core pillars of trust: **Body Language, Motives, Integrity, Skillset, and Track Record.** Each of these plays a crucial role in determining whether someone is perceived as trustworthy or not.

1. Assign Scores for Each Category (1 to 10)

For each of the five categories, you'll assign a score based on real-world observations. Trust is about behavior, and behavior leaves clues.

- **Body Language (1-10):** Are they avoiding eye contact, fidgeting, or presenting a disheveled appearance? Closed-off or inconsistent body language can signal distrust.
- **Motives (1-10):** Do they have a hidden agenda, seem manipulative, or frequently change their stance? People trust those with clear and honest intentions.
- **Integrity (1-10):** Do they break promises, act dishonestly,

or avoid accountability? If so, their integrity score drops fast.

- **Skillset (1-10):** Are they actually capable of delivering on their promises? This includes experience, performance, communication, and handling challenges.
- **Track Record (1-10):** What does their history look like? A strong track-record builds confidence; repeated failures create doubt.

A word of caution on scoring: I strongly recommend you **never give someone a 10** in any category unless you've had the opportunity to **observe their behavior consistently for at least 3 to 6 months.** Trust is built on what people *do*, not what they *say*. A 10 is earned—not assumed.

Someone once said, *"Never judge a person by their worst or best achievement. Score them on what you see repeated again and again."* That's the spirit behind this system. Give people room to earn trust through patterns, not promises. And if you're handing out 9s or 10s too quickly, you're not scoring trust—you're projecting hope.

(SC) I had to look at myself through this exact lens. In the early days after my resignation, my integrity was scored low. My motives were under scrutiny. My track record? It wasn't gone—but it had a major dent. The only way back was to go score by score and start rebuilding. I

> didn't just apologize—I had to demonstrate, day
> after day, that I could be trusted again.

2. Use the Trust Scale

Once you've rated each category, you classify them into one of three trust tiers:

T (I Trust them is a 7-10)

- They exhibit strong trustworthiness in this area. While no one is perfect, they've given you little reason to doubt them.

Q (I Question their Trustworthiness is a 4-6)

- This is the danger zone. Some red flags have popped up, but trust isn't completely destroyed—yet.

CF (Critical Failure in Trust is a 1-3)

- They've repeatedly demonstrated behavior that breaks trust. This could be through dishonesty, incompetence, or a complete lack of reliability.

3. Calculate the Trust Credit Score (Crash)

Once you've assigned scores to each of the five categories, it's time to calculate the overall score.

- Add up all five scores.
- Divide the total by five to get the **average score**.

What Your Score Means

Your final Trust Credit Score (Crash) tells you how fractured trust really is and what level of repair is needed:

- **1-3:** *Highly Fractured Trust*—Major issues. This level indicates that trust is almost nonexistent, and major work is required to restore it. Immediate action is needed if the relationship is to be salvaged.
- **4-6:** *Moderate Trust Issues*—There's still a foundation, but trust has been weakened. Repair is possible, but it will require intentional effort and consistent action.
- **7-10:** *Minimal Trust Issues*—Trust is mostly intact, but there are some concerns that need addressing before they escalate.

Why This Matters

When trust is broken, people tend to react emotionally, either over-reacting or dismissing the problem altogether. But with the Crash scoring system, trust becomes measurable. Instead of saying, *"I don't trust this person,"* you can say, *"Their integrity score is low, and their track record is shaky. If they want to rebuild trust, they need to follow through on commitments and demonstrate consistency."*

  This system provides clarity. It takes the guesswork out of trust repair and allows individuals and teams to identify exactly where the fractures are. More importantly, it empowers them to fix it.

The Path to Trust Recovery

Once you know *why* trust is broken, you can focus on solutions. If someone's integrity score is low, they need to prove themselves through honesty and accountability. If their skillset is the issue, they may need training or mentorship. If their motives are unclear, transparent communication can help rebuild confidence.

> When I was rebuilding my own life and career, I had to take ownership in every category. I had to demonstrate integrity over time. I had to be consistent. I had to deliver results in a new arena—business coaching—where no one knew my name or history. Slowly but surely, my scores rose. And with that came new relationships, new opportunities, and a new platform of trust that I could stand on again.

The best part? The Trust Credit Score (Crash) model isn't just for calling people out—it's a blueprint for **trust transformation**. If trust is your currency, this system is your financial planner, helping you make smarter trust investments, cut your losses, and maximize your ROI on relationships.

In the end, trust isn't about perfection. It's about predictability. When you know how to measure trust, you can manage it. And when you can manage trust, you can accelerate cooperation, success, and connection—faster than ever before.

Trust Credit Score™ (Crash)

DECLINED

How BAD Is It - (1-10)

6 **①** **Their Vibe Is Out of Sync | Body Language**
Avoiding Eye Contact / Fidgeting / Closed Posture / Inconsistent Facial Expressions / Disheveled Appearance

7 **②** **Something Feels Shady | Motives**
Hidden Agendas / Manipulative Behavior / Frequent Changes / Conflict of Interest / Vague Statements

5 **③** **Their Actions Don't Add Up | Integrity**
Conflicted Values / Breaks Promises / Inconsistent Actions / Dishonesty / Avoids Accountability

8 **④** **Are They Even Built for This | Skillset**
Lack of Experience / Inconsistent Performance / Limited Skill Set / Poor Communication / Low Curiosity and Avoidance of Challenges

6 **⑤** **I'm Not Seeing Any Receipts | Wins**
Frequent Failures / Incomplete Projects / Negative Feedback / Short Tenure / Lack of Notable Achievements

32 / 5 = **6.4**

Scott@ScottCarley.com ✉
TrustEnergizer.com ✆
512-470-0570 ☎

THE CHANGE ENERGIZER

CHAPTER 12

How to Have a Courageous Conversation

Courageous Conversations: The Key to Correcting the Problem and Restoring Trust

Every great performance has a script, a cast, and a director who ensures that everyone stays in character. In the workplace, **trust is the invisible currency that determines whether a team thrives or stumbles.** But what happens when someone goes "off script"—when their actions break trust, slow down cooperation, or create friction?

This is where **Courageous Conversations** come in. **This is the hard part—the real, actionable step that corrects the problem and gets your team back on track.** You can talk about leadership principles all day long, but unless you have the courage to address underperformance, misalignment, or trust fractures, the system won't work. **This is the chapter that makes the Trust Credit Score™ come alive.**

Why We Avoid the Hard Conversations

Let's be honest: most people dread difficult conversations.

- Fear of conflict and confrontation. Many people worry that addressing performance issues will lead to tension, arguments, or damaged relationships. The discomfort of potential conflict often causes leaders to hesitate or delay the conversation altogether.

- Fear of hurting someone's feelings. Leaders want to be supportive, but they also need to ensure that team members meet expectations. Balancing honesty with sensitivity can feel like walking a tightrope.

- Fear of backlash or pushback. It's common to anticipate resistance, especially when giving critical feedback. People may become defensive, emotional, or even retaliate by disengaging further.

- Fear of making the situation worse. Sometimes, addressing an issue improperly can escalate tensions rather than resolve them. Without a structured approach, many leaders feel uncertain about how to navigate these conversations effectively.

But avoiding the conversation only deepens the problem. **Silence doesn't fix trust issues—it compounds them.**

Yet, what if I told you there's a way to make these tough conversations **easier, more effective, and even transformational?** What if you had a framework that takes the fear out of addressing underperformance and helps you actually improve trust instead of damaging it further?

The Disney Approach: Casting Calls and Staying in Character

At Disney, every job opening is a **Casting Call** because employees aren't just workers—they are **cast members** playing a role in a larger production. Whether they are in guest services, finance, or operations, everyone has a role to play in delivering the magic. **And when someone stops playing their role correctly, they need a reminder to get back into character.**

This same approach applies to **trust and performance** in any workplace. When a team member isn't operating in alignment with trust-building behaviors—whether through poor communication, lack of accountability, or failing to follow through on commitments—they have stepped "out of character."

As a leader, your job is to **coach, not condemn.** Instead of attacking or avoiding the issue, **your role is to guide them back**

into the trusted version of themselves. And that starts with one key phrase:

"**How can I help you get back into character with regards to these points on the Trust Credit Score?**"

This simple yet powerful question shifts the conversation from **confrontation to collaboration**. It makes the person feel seen, heard, and supported while still holding them accountable.

The Chapter That Can Turn Your Department Around

The strategies in this chapter will equip you with the tools to have Courageous Conversations without fear. These aren't theoretical concepts—they are the real-world tactics that can change how your team operates, how trust is restored, and how performance skyrockets.

By following these steps, you'll:

- Address underperformance without creating resentment. Leaders who master this approach can confront issues constructively, ensuring that the team member feels supported rather than attacked.

- Restore broken trust and increase cooperation. When people understand that conversations are about improvement, not punishment, they are more likely to engage in productive dialogue.

- Help your team members realign with their best selves. Courageous Conversations remind individuals of their strengths and capabilities while guiding them back to behaviors that build trust.

- Turn avoidance into action, making conversations easier and more productive. The longer issues are ignored, the more they fester. This framework helps leaders take decisive, confident action without unnecessary hesitation.

If you master this, you will transform your leadership. Because at the end of the day, trust isn't built in the easy moments—it's built in the moments when you choose to have the conversation that others avoid.

Framework for Courageous Conversations

Opening the Conversation:

"Are you OK?"

Genuine Concern: "Michael, how are you doing? I genuinely want to check in. What's been your biggest frustration recently? You seem a little out of character." This sets a tone of empathy and curiosity, signaling that you care about their well-being before diving into the performance issues.

The 7-Step Framework:

1. **Listen First:**
- **Why:** People feel valued when they are heard, and it opens the door for trust. Employees who feel like their

perspective matters are more willing to engage in constructive conversations.

- **How:** Ask open-ended questions to let them express in their own words. "What's been weighing you down recently?" This helps uncover underlying issues, such as personal challenges or workplace frustrations, that may be impacting their performance.

2. **Use Good Timing:**

- **Why:** Timing is everything. Address the issue while it's still relevant but not overly emotional. Bringing it up too soon can make someone feel attacked, while waiting too long can let resentment build.

- **How:** Choose a moment when the person is receptive and not overwhelmed, such as during a one-on-one meeting or at a time when they seem more relaxed and open to discussion.

3. **Affirm Their Value:**

- **Why:** When people know they are valued, they are more open to correction. If they feel like they are just being criticized, they may shut down or become defensive.

- **How:** "I know you have the company's best interests at heart, and your contributions are valuable." Reinforcing their worth while addressing concerns fosters a growth mindset instead of fear.

4. **Do Your Research (Be Prepared):**

- **Why:** Grounding feedback in facts shows your concerns

are objective, not personal. Without solid evidence, the conversation may feel like an opinion-based attack rather than a constructive discussion.

- **How:** Review their Trust Credit Score and KPIs before the conversation. Be ready with specific examples of behaviors or results that need improvement, so the discussion is clear and productive.

5. **Confront Reality and Talk Straight:**

- **Why:** Avoid sugarcoating or vague feedback. Clarity prevents confusion and enables real progress.
- **How:** "We need to talk about how this is affecting the team's trust. It's out of character for you, and it's impacting our speed of cooperation." Being direct while staying supportive is key.

6. **Prepare for Objections and Pushback:**

- **Why:** Resistance is natural, especially when someone feels challenged. Some may react defensively or try to shift blame.
- **How:** "I hear what you're saying, but we can't ignore the impact this is having on trust and collaboration. Let's address it together." Acknowledge their perspective but keep the focus on solutions.

7. **Get Them Back Into Character:**

- **Why:** Help them reconnect with their best self—the version that aligns with trust-building behaviors.

- **How:** "Let's get you back to the version of yourself that I know and trust." Encourage ownership and improvement in a way that motivates rather than discourages.

By grounding the conversation in empathy, facts, and a shared goal of getting "back in character," you're not just addressing performance issues—you're reinforcing their identity and value to the team.

Role-playing Activities

Role-playing activities can be powerful in helping team members practice Courageous Conversations. Here are a few two-person role-play scenarios to guide participants in exercising these skills, focusing on trust, feedback, and performance improvement:

1. The "Out of Character" Conversation

- **Scenario:** One person plays a manager, and the other plays an underperforming team member who has been "out of character" based on the Trust Credit Score (e.g., missed deadlines, lack of initiative, or poor communication).
- **Objective:** The manager will initiate a Courageous Conversation to bring the underperformer back "in character," using empathy, observation, and clear feedback.

Steps:

- Manager starts by expressing genuine concern: "Hey [Name], how are you feeling? I noticed you seem a little out of character lately."

- Underperformer responds with their frustrations or reasons for the behavior.
- Manager listens, affirms their value, and brings up specific observations about how their performance has impacted trust and the team.
- Both discuss how to move forward and "get back in character."

Debrief Questions:

- How did the manager balance empathy and direct feedback?
- How did the underperformer react to being confronted, and how did they feel during the conversation?
- Was the issue resolved constructively? What could have been handled differently?

2. Handling Objections

- **Scenario:** One person plays a manager, and the other plays a defensive team member who pushes back against feedback (e.g., shifting blame, denying responsibility, or becoming emotional).
- **Objective:** The manager must navigate objections, listen empathetically, and help the team member understand the need for change while maintaining trust and open communication.

Steps:

- Manager delivers a specific piece of feedback about

performance (e.g., "I noticed you've missed several dead-lines recently, and it's creating delays for the team").

- The team member objects (e.g., "I've had too much on my plate, and no one else is stepping up").
- Manager practices staying calm, acknowledging the concern, and reiterating the need to address the issue (e.g., "I understand things have been overwhelming, but we need to find a solution that helps the team move forward").

Debrief Questions:

- How did the manager handle objections? Did they maintain the balance between empathy and accountability?
- How could they better address the root cause of the defensiveness?

3. Affirming Value and Confronting Reality

- **Scenario:** One person plays the manager, and the other plays a team member who feels undervalued or unappreciated, leading to disengagement and lack of effort.
- **Objective:** The manager affirms the team member's value, listens to their concerns, and confronts the reality of their underperformance with respect and clarity.

Steps:

- Manager begins by affirming the team member's value:

"I want you to know how much we appreciate the work you've done here. You're a key part of the team."

- The team member expresses feelings of being overlooked or undervalued.
- Manager listens, then transitions to discussing how their disengagement has been affecting the team's progress and trust (e.g., "I hear that you feel underappreciated, but we need to address how this is affecting team collaboration and results").

Debrief Questions:

- Did the affirmation of value help the team member feel seen and heard?
- How could the manager balance recognizing emotions and maintaining focus on performance improvement?

4. Courageous Conversation with a Peer

- **Scenario:** Two colleagues have been clashing, and one has noticed trust is being broken due to miscommunication or conflicting behaviors. One person plays the colleague initiating the conversation, and the other plays the peer who has been difficult to work with.
- **Objective:** The team member will practice initiating a Courageous Conversation with a peer by discussing how behaviors are breaking trust and affecting the team's cooperation.

Steps:

- Initiating team member starts with empathy: "Hey [Name], I've noticed some friction between us lately, and I think it's affecting how we collaborate."
- Peer responds by either acknowledging or dismissing the concern.
- Initiating team member listens, then discusses how specific behaviors have fractured trust and asks how they can work better together moving forward.

Debrief Questions:

- How did the initiating team member handle bringing up a tough issue with a peer?
- Was the conversation constructive and respectful, even if there were disagreements?

5. Confronting Motive and Integrity Issues

- **Scenario:** One person plays a manager, and the other plays a team member whose actions have been misaligned with company values or motives (e.g., withholding information, taking shortcuts, or prioritizing self-interest over team goals).
- **Objective:** The manager will address issues of motive or integrity and guide the team member back into alignment with the company's core values.

Steps:

- Manager brings up the specific behavior: "I've noticed that lately, some of your decisions seem out of sync with our core values—like when you [describe the behavior]."
- Team member explains their reasoning or justifies the actions.
- Manager listens, then emphasizes the importance of integrity and values: "Our team's trust depends on us acting in line with our shared values. Can we work on aligning your actions with those values again?"

Debrief Questions:

- How well did the manager address the trust and integrity issue?
- Was the conversation effective in helping the team member understand the impact of their behavior?

These role-play scenarios allow participants to practice handling difficult conversations in a safe, structured way. Each scenario focuses on different aspects of Courageous Conversations—listening, addressing objections, affirming value, and confronting difficult truths—while keeping the ultimate goal of restoring trust and performance at the forefront.

CHAPTER 13

The Significance of Two Perspectives

The idea of having two separate perspectives—**Trust Credit Score™ (Positive)** and **Trust Credit Score™ (Crash)**—is highly significant for several reasons. Each perspective serves a distinct purpose and allows for a more **comprehensive, dynamic understanding of trust** in various professional and personal situations. Here's why this dual approach is important:

1. Holistic Trust Management

- **Positive Trust Score** focuses on recognizing and nurturing trust-building behaviors, creating a positive feedback loop. It allows individuals or teams to see where they are excelling and how to continue reinforcing trust.
- **Crash Trust Score** gives you a tool to address fractured trust. Trust breakdowns are inevitable in long-term relationships or teams, and this perspective helps diagnose and repair the damage rather than letting it fester.

Significance: Trust is not static—it fluctuates based on behavior, performance, and communication. Having two models ensures you're not just measuring trust when things are going well but also knowing what to do when it's compromised. This creates a full-cycle trust management process.

2. Proactive vs. Reactive

- **Proactive**: The positive model encourages continuous improvement. By regularly assessing trust in high-functioning teams or individuals, leaders can take proactive steps to strengthen trust before problems arise.
- **Reactive**: The crash model comes into play when trust has already been damaged. It helps quickly identify specific trust issues and provide a roadmap for corrective action.

Significance: In many environments, people only address trust when it's already broken, which is often too late. Having both perspectives allows leaders to proactively maintain high trust levels while also having a clear, structured way to handle crises when they occur. This leads to better long-term outcomes and more resilient relationships.

3. Different Tools for Different Contexts

- **Positive**: You use the positive perspective to recognize and reward strong relationships, behaviors, and team dynamics. It's helpful in feedback sessions, team evaluations, or leadership assessments.
- **Crash**: The crash model provides an essential tool for crisis management or conflict resolution. It's most useful after a specific event where trust has clearly been damaged, whether it's a missed deadline, a failed project, or interpersonal conflict.

Significance: Each tool fits a particular context. Without the crash model, leaders may struggle to address trust-related problems because they don't have a structured way to diagnose the issue. Without the positive model, they may miss out on opportunities to nurture and grow trust before problems arise.

4. Encourages Accountability and Growth

- **Positive**: Reinforces positive behaviors and habits. It allows people to celebrate their successes and build on them.

- **Crash**: Encourages accountability when things go wrong. By scoring poor behaviors or actions that led to fractured trust, it helps individuals or teams take responsibility for their actions and find a path to rebuild trust.

Significance: Both perspectives foster a **growth mindset** around trust. One recognizes strengths, and the other helps address weaknesses, allowing for continuous improvement in personal development and team dynamics.

5. Promotes Self-Awareness

- **Positive**: This perspective allows individuals to understand their strengths in building trust, giving them confidence and validation in their relationships or leadership.
- **Crash**: This perspective forces self-awareness in areas where trust is being undermined. By using clear, actionable criteria, it helps people see where they've gone wrong and what they can do to fix it.

Significance: Self-awareness is critical for growth, and these two models provide a complete picture. Without both perspectives, there would be a gap in understanding trust fully—people might not realize how fragile trust can be, nor how powerful it is when maintained.

6. Supports a Culture of Open Communication

- **Positive**: Encourages frequent check-ins and discussions about trust, making it a regular part of organizational culture.
- **Crash**: When trust breaks down, having a model to address it encourages open, honest conversations about what went wrong and how to move forward.

Significance: Having both perspectives ensures that communication about trust doesn't just happen during good times but also when there are issues. It makes it easier to navigate difficult conversations and creates a culture where trust can be openly discussed and improved.

7. Prevents Long-Term Damage

- **Positive**: Helps maintain high trust, which leads to better cooperation, faster decision-making, and stronger relationships.
- **Crash**: By catching and addressing fractured trust early, this model prevents small issues from snowballing into long-term damage that could cripple a team or relationship.

Significance: Without the crash model, fractured trust can go unaddressed and worsen over time, leading to deeper issues. The positive model helps prevent issues from arising by maintaining high trust levels. Together, they create a preventive and corrective trust framework.

Conclusion: The Importance of Two Perspectives

The dual perspective of **Trust Credit Score (Positive)** and **Trust Credit Score (Crash)** is significant because it equips leaders, teams, and individuals with a **comprehensive toolset** to manage trust at every stage—whether trust is thriving or has been fractured. This balanced approach encourages both proactive trust-building and reactive trust-repairing strategies, ultimately leading to stronger, more resilient relationships and teams.

In essence, these two perspectives cover the full lifecycle of trust—**building it, maintaining it, and repairing it when necessary**—making it a crucial framework for anyone interested in personal or professional development, leadership, or team dynamics.

CHAPTER 14

How to Use the Two Perspective Model

To effectively use each of these **Trust Credit Score** modules—both the **positive version** and the **crash version**—for different perspectives, you can guide people to focus on specific situations where trust is either strong or broken. Here's a breakdown of how to instruct people on when and how to use each model:

1. Positive Trust Credit Score™ Model (The Strengths)

Purpose: Use this model when evaluating a person, team, or organization that is functioning well and you want to reinforce or recognize trust-building behaviors. This model helps identify areas where trust is strong and provides insight into maintaining and enhancing that trust.

Instructions:

- **Who should use it**: Managers, team leaders, mentors, and anyone evaluating a high-functioning team member or colleague.

- **When to use it**: During regular performance reviews, team assessments, or when preparing for leadership decisions like promotions or additional responsibilities.

How to use it:

- Ask the individual to self-assess or have their peers score them using the five categories: Body Language, Motives, Integrity, Skillset, and Track Record.

- Use this model to give constructive feedback by highlighting where the individual is already performing well.

- Share the score with the person or team and discuss ways to maintain high trust levels and improve any weaker areas.

Example: Use this model when considering a candidate for a leadership position, focusing on their ability to build trust with their team.

2. Trust Credit Score™ (Crash Version–The Fractures)

Purpose: This model is for evaluating situations where trust has been damaged. It helps identify the specific behaviors or areas causing distrust, allowing for focused efforts to rebuild that trust.

Instructions:

- **Who should use it**: Managers, team leaders, or individuals dealing with fractured relationships, either with colleagues, clients, or teams.
- **When to use it**: After a conflict, failure to deliver on promises, or when relationships in the workplace are suffering from a lack of cooperation or communication.

How to use it:

- Score the individual or situation using the five categories from the **Crash** model: Body Language, Motives, Integrity, Skillset, and Track Record. Focus on identifying specific red flags like inconsistent body language, hidden agendas, or poor performance.
- Use the scores as a diagnostic tool to start a constructive conversation about the root causes of the fractured trust.
- Prioritize addressing the lowest-scoring areas to begin rebuilding trust. This might include coaching on body

language, transparency around motives, or a commitment to greater accountability.

Example: Use this model after a key team member misses deadlines repeatedly, causing the team to lose faith in their ability to contribute. Assess where trust broke down and how they can begin to recover it.

How to Tell People to Use the Modules Based on Their Perspectives

For Leaders/Managers:

- **Positive Module**: "Use this to recognize and reward trust-building behaviors in your team. By assessing body language, motives, integrity, skillset, and track record, you'll identify strengths that you can amplify across the organization."
- **Crash Module**: "When you're seeing poor cooperation, slow decision-making, or fractured relationships, use the Crash Model. It helps you pinpoint specific areas where trust is failing, so you can address them directly and start the recovery process."

For Team Members/Employees:

- **Positive Module**: "Self-assess using this tool to understand how well you're building trust with your colleagues. It can give you insights into where you're excelling and what you can do to further strengthen your work relationships."

- **Crash Module**: "If you feel like your actions have led to a loss of trust with your peers or manager, use this model to assess where things went wrong. It can guide you to understand which behaviors are undermining trust and give you a path to make things right."

For Coaches/Consultants:

Positive Module: "This is a great tool to assess the strengths of your clients in building trust, especially when they're striving for leadership roles. You can use this during regular reviews to help them enhance their interpersonal and leadership skills."

Crash Module: "Use this as a recovery tool with clients whose teams are struggling. It's a diagnostic model that allows you to address specific trust issues in the workplace, coaching them through how to rebuild trust."

Practical Tip for Both Modules:

Encourage people to use these tools consistently. Trust is dynamic, and evaluating it regularly using these models can help maintain high performance and smooth operations, whether it's in a leadership capacity or day-to-day teamwork.

By framing the modules as **proactive (positive)** or **reactive (crash)**, people can decide which model best suits their current situation and how to apply it for maximum impact.

PART IV

Beyond the Workplace

CHAPTER 15

Reputation Rehab

How to Rebuild Trust at Work and in Life

Let's be real—your reputation is everything.

In every workplace, team, or friend group, reputation is the quiet force that either opens doors or shuts them. It's not about your title. It's not about your resume. It's not even about how nice your LinkedIn profile looks. It's about how people feel when your name comes up in the room—and you're not in it.

Reputation is the **emotional shortcut** people use to decide:

Can I trust you? Can I count on you? Do I want to work with you—or do I need to brace myself when you're involved?

That's why your reputation isn't a background detail—it's your **Trust Credit Score**™ **in motion.** It's your street-level brand, your day-to-day credibility, and your silent advantage—or disadvantage.

The Trust Credit Score™ – Your Reputation Report Card

Your **Trust Credit Score**™ is a direct reflection of your **reputation in action**. It measures how reliable, consistent, and competent people perceive you to be. And just like a financial credit score, it's built slowly, but it can drop fast.

You build trust with **repeatable, observable behavior.** And you break it with the same.

Take Jeanette. She's that teammate who's always early, double-checks her work, and brings positive energy into the room. She doesn't just get the job done—she raises the standard. No drama, no excuses. People know they can rely on her, which means she's constantly invited into bigger rooms, better projects, and real opportunities. Her Trust Credit Score™ is in excellent standing.

Then there's Rosie. She's smart, yes—but unreliable. She's late more often than not. Her work is last-minute and full of small mistakes. She's forgetful, and her follow-up game is weak. Even when she *wants* to contribute, her reputation precedes her. Over time, the team stops counting on her. She gets passed over. Not because people dislike her—but because they don't *trust* her.

That's the power of a reputation. It travels faster than you do. And it speaks louder than any pitch, apology, or performance review.

I experienced that power firsthand when I had to rebuild not just a reputation—but a life. After losing my role as a senior pastor and my ministerial license, I stepped into a season of public failure. The weight of that loss followed me everywhere. My marriage ended, my career path collapsed, and the community that once celebrated me now questioned every move I made. I remember walking into rooms where I used to be welcomed—and feeling the shift. It wasn't hate. It was distrust. And it was earned.

Reputation is Built Through Behavior, Not Intention

You may *mean* well. You may even have talent. But none of that matters if the people around you are constantly cleaning up after your missed deadlines, unclear communication, or no-show behavior. In other words, **your good intentions don't count if your execution breaks trust.**

Here's the flip side: **you don't have to be perfect to be trusted.** You just have to be consistent. You can have flaws and still have a high Trust Credit Score™ if you're honest, dependable, and you follow through on what matters.

Trust is earned with patterns, not promises. And when those

patterns break down, **Reputation Rehab** becomes your only way forward.

> I couldn't fix my reputation with one conversation or one apology. I had to reintroduce myself to the world through action. When I transitioned into business, no one knew who I had been—and that was a gift. I wasn't trying to hide my past. I was focused on proving, through behavior, that I could be counted on. It started with small workshops, one-on-one coaching sessions, showing up every week to networking events. No flair. No hype. Just value, consistency, and humility. That's how trust started to flow again.

Rebuilding Trust: The Rosie Redemption Story

After too many late arrivals and missed commitments, Rosie got called into a second PIP meeting. This was it. The decision point.

Keep making excuses—or get serious about change.

Rosie chose rehab.

She started small: setting two alarms, prepping her day the night before, confirming meetings the day of. She over-communicated and asked for feedback. She didn't just show up on time—she showed up ready. Over time, her coworkers started to notice. The eye rolls stopped. The confidence came back. And eventually, so did the opportunities.

Reputation Rehab works. But it's not a one-off apology. It's a **repatterning**—a new, visible way of operating.

Your Reputation Rehab Plan

If your Trust Credit Score™ is dragging and your reputation could use a reset, here's where you start. These five steps aren't just checkboxes—they're behavior shifts that rebuild credibility, one interaction at a time.

1. Own Your Mistakes

Stop spinning the story. Don't deflect. Don't blame the system, the inbox, the weather, or Mercury in retrograde.

Own it. Fix it. Move forward.

When you take responsibility without drama, people are often more forgiving than you think. But they need to see that you're self-aware—and serious about improvement.

Pro move: Address the impact of the mistake, not just the cause. That's what shows maturity.

When I confessed my failure, I didn't hide behind excuses. I stepped down. I submitted to wise counsel. And I told the truth—to

> my wife, my board, and the people I had let down.
> That decision didn't fix everything, but it created
> the starting point for recovery. Ownership was
> the first deposit in my rebuilt Trust Credit Score™.

2. Show Up Consistently

Reputation is about repetition. That means **being present, prepared, and predictable** in the best way. When people know what version of you is going to show up—and that it's your best one—they start trusting you again.

Pro move: Don't just show up—*re-engage.* Ask questions. Add value. Let people feel your commitment, not just your attendance.

3. Exceed Expectations

Want to fast-track trust recovery? **Over-deliver without over-explaining.**

Complete your work early. Bring insights, not just output. Take initiative on the little things. These micro-wins build momentum and remind people why they believed in you in the first place.

Pro move: Don't make a big show of it. Let the work speak. Quiet consistency is powerful.

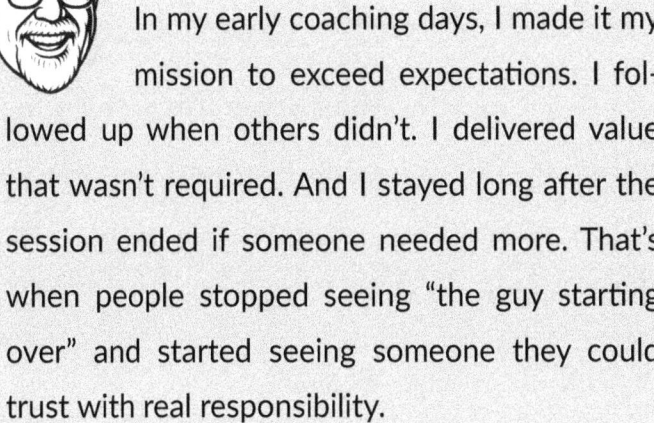

In my early coaching days, I made it my mission to exceed expectations. I followed up when others didn't. I delivered value that wasn't required. And I stayed long after the session ended if someone needed more. That's when people stopped seeing "the guy starting over" and started seeing someone they could trust with real responsibility.

4. Improve Your Communication

Silence erodes trust faster than failure.

Even if you're still figuring things out, **keep people in the loop.** Let them know where things stand, what's next, and how you're addressing potential issues.

Pro move: Communicate before you're asked. Anticipation builds confidence.

5. Shift Your Mindset

You're not just fixing a flaw—you're building a new identity. That means trading victim language for solution language. It means asking, "What's my next right move?" instead of "Why does this always happen to me?"

Pro move: Let your energy speak before your words do. Show up like you're already trusted—and act in a way that keeps it.

Reality Check: What's Your Reputation Saying When You're Not Around?

Here's a simple exercise: Think about five people you interact with regularly at work. What's the first word that comes to mind for each of them? Now flip it—what's the first word that comes to mind when *they* think of *you?*

- Dependable or unpredictable?
- Positive or draining?
- Capable or high-maintenance?

Your reputation is built one behavior at a time. And while it may take weeks or months to shift perception, **it only takes one moment of integrity to begin the rebuild.**

Final Thought: Your Reputation Is Your Resume

In today's world, your reputation travels faster than your work does. People will talk about you before your emails get opened. They'll make trust-based decisions about you before the meeting even starts.

That's why **Reputation Rehab isn't optional—it's strategic.**

And if your Trust Credit Score™ needs a reboot, the good news is: you don't need to wait for permission. You just need to act differently—consistently.

> Today, I'm trusted. Not because of a clean record—but because I did the work. I took the long road. I lived the five pillars. And I rebuilt my Trust Credit Score™ one decision, one relationship, one behavior at a time. If I can do it, you can too.

Because trust may be fragile, but it's also renewable.

And when you build it back, **you don't just get restored—you get upgraded.**

CHAPTER 16

How to Rebuild Trust Within the Family

How the Trust Credit Score™ Can Strengthen Our Vibes at Home

Trust is the secret sauce that makes our family relationships click. But even in the tightest of fams, sometimes we need a little structure to keep everything on track—enter the Trust Credit Score™ System. This isn't just some corporate strategy; it's a real-deal way to amp up the trust within our own home squad.

Breaking Down the Trust Credit Score™ System

This system focuses on five key areas that can make or break the trust vibes at home:

1. **Appearance and Body Language:** How we show up matters—even at home. Keeping things open, like actually looking up from your phone and making eye contact, can send signals that you're here, present, and trustworthy.

2. **Motives and Intentions:** Ever wonder why your sibling suddenly wants to do you a favor? Yeah, getting clear on why we do what we do helps everyone feel more secure. No hidden agendas here, just keeping it 100.

3. **Core Values and Integrity:** This is about walking the talk. We all have our family values, whether it's honesty, support, or respect. Living up to these consistently builds massive trust.

4. **Skillset:** Whether it's nailing your chores or smashing your schoolwork, showing you can handle your biz reassures everyone that you're reliable.

5. **Track Record:** Trust isn't built overnight. It's all about what you've done day in, day out. Keeping your word and staying consistent are key.

How to Implement It

- **Chat It Out:** Regular fam jams can help everyone feel heard and clarify any trust issues. It's about building a safe space where everyone can spill the tea honestly.

- **Expectation Station:** Set clear expectations for everyone in the household. From who unloads the dishwasher to how we handle a timeout after a heated game night—clarity is king.

- **Keep It Real:** Feedback is essential. Whether it's a quick check-in or a more formal sit-down, talk about what's working and what's not without any drama.

- **Sort It Out:** When there's beef, don't let it stew. Address issues fairly and swiftly to keep the trust tank full.

- **Own Your Oops:** Messed up? Own it. Apologize sincerely and learn from it. This shows you're serious about keeping things tight.

- **Team Up:** Dive into activities that need teamwork. Whether it's a puzzle night or a DIY home project, doing things together strengthens bonds.

- **Lead by Example:** Parents, this one's on you. Show 'em how it's done with your own actions. Kids notice everything, and they'll mirror what they see.

- **Positive Props:** Recognize when someone goes above and beyond in the trust department. A little praise can go a long way.

Wrapping It Up

The Trust Credit Score™ isn't just another tool—it's a way to make sure everyone in the family feels secure, valued, and connected. By focusing on how we show up for each other every day, we can build a home vibe that's all about support and trust. Let's keep it strong, keep it real, and turn our fam into an even tighter crew.

CHAPTER 17

TCS is *Not a Weapon*

The Trust Credit Score: A Tool, Not a Weapon

I n the professional world, trust is a currency we spend daily. The Trust Credit Score™ was designed as a powerful tool to help leaders, teams, and individuals evaluate where trust stands in their relationships. But like any tool, it can be misused. Just as you wouldn't use a measuring tape to criticize someone's height, the Trust Credit Score isn't a tool for nit-picking or weaponizing interpersonal dynamics. Here's why it's essential to keep the Trust Credit Score constructive, not destructive.

1. Understanding the Trust Credit Score's Purpose

The Trust Credit Score serves as a guide to understanding and improving the quality of trust within teams and relationships. It helps identify strengths and weaknesses in areas such as motives, integrity, and results. However, it's not about punishment or judgment—it's about growth. Used thoughtfully, this tool can empower you to build stronger, more transparent relationships. Misused, it risks becoming a source of resentment and division.

2. Avoiding "Double Trouble" with the Trust Credit Score

Weaponizing the Trust Credit Score can create a cycle of what we call "Double Trouble." Imagine a scenario where someone's low score is repeatedly brought up in meetings as a point of criticism, or trust "scores" become gossip fodder around the water cooler. This doesn't just harm the individual; it harms the team's culture. Trust fractures can deepen, and people become reluctant to communicate openly, fearing judgment or backlash.

Instead, use the Trust Credit Score constructively by focusing on growth and mutual improvement. Instead of calling out a team member for "low trust," initiate a supportive conversation: "Here's an area where we can grow together." This approach builds resilience instead of defensiveness.

3. The Downside of Weaponizing Transparency

Transparency is one of the Trust Credit Score's core strengths, but when weaponized, it can become a liability. Suppose someone's trust score in a particular area, like integrity or motives, is consistently brought up. This could lead to a toxic culture where people feel they're always under a microscope, leading to reduced morale and innovation.

Transparency must be balanced with empathy. Approach feedback with a mindset of understanding rather than judgment. Ask questions and listen. Rather than condemning someone based on a single score, use it to open a dialogue about improvement and support.

4. Fostering a Growth Mindset, Not a Blame Game

In a growth-oriented culture, every member of the team is working toward a common goal. The Trust Credit Score should reflect this shared mission. If a score reveals a challenge, it should become an opportunity for collective problem-solving rather than individual blame. Make it a collaborative effort to raise everyone's scores and build a stronger, more cohesive team.

5. Remember: The Trust Credit Score is a Compass, Not a Weapon

Ultimately, the Trust Credit Score is a guide. It can point you toward areas that need improvement, but it should never be used to wound or control. Leaders must model this by using the Trust Credit Score as a means to enhance understanding, boost morale, and encourage growth—not as a metric for punishment or exclusion.

The Trust Credit Score™ has immense potential to elevate teams and relationships when used with care and empathy. By treating it as a tool for growth, you create an environment where trust flourishes, people feel valued, and everyone wins. So next time you consider someone's score, ask yourself: Am I using this as a compass to guide us forward, or as a weapon that could set us back?

PART V

Trust
That Lasts

CHAPTER 18

The Trust Credit Score™

Your New Culture Code

This isn't just a good idea.

This is your next competitive edge.

If you've made it this far, you've seen the power of trust in every part of life and leadership. Trust accelerates collaboration. It opens doors. It gets people to follow you, buy from you, promote you, and believe in you.

But more than anything else, trust gives you **leverage**—because when people trust you, they stop second-guessing and start aligning. That's where the magic happens. And that's where this system comes alive.

The Trust Credit Score™ isn't just a framework. It's a **culture code.** It's a way to raise the bar—not just for yourself, but for your team, your company, your relationships, and every interaction you lead.

Trust Is the New Scoreboard

Let's be real—most businesses have no system for assessing trust. They rely on gut feelings, hearsay, and whether someone "seems like a good fit." That's a risky way to run a business.

When you install the Trust Credit Score™ mindset, you create a **shared language** and **standard of behavior** that removes the guesswork.

Instead of wondering:

- Why aren't people following that leader?
- Why is the sales cycle stalling?
- Why does this team feel stuck?

You can ask the real questions:

- Where is trust strong?
- Where is trust fractured?
- How can we raise the score?

How to Bring This Into Your Culture

Here's how to start putting it into motion, one layer at a time.

1. Assess Yourself First

You can't lead trust if you're not practicing it. Take yourself through the full TCS process—both the standard score and the Crash model. Identify the pillar you need to improve, and commit to rebuilding it with observable behavior.

Ask yourself weekly: What's one action I can take to raise my Trust Credit Score™?

2. Teach the Five Trust Signals

Introduce your team to the five areas where trust is gained or lost:

- Body Language – What vibe are we giving off?
- Motives – Are we clear and upfront?
- Values – Are we aligned with what we say we stand for?
- Skillset – Can we actually do what we say?
- Track Record – Are we consistent over time?

You don't have to explain everything at once—just start using the language. Once the team has the language, they'll start building the behavior.

3. Make Trust Measurable

Use simple scoring (1–10) in reviews, check-ins, and post-project evaluations. Normalize talking about trust the way we talk about results. When trust becomes visible, it becomes actionable.

4. Have Courageous Conversations

When someone's falling out of character, don't let it fester. Use the casting call language and invite them back into alignment. Address the issue early with clarity and kindness—because trust that's caught early is easier to restore.

5. Celebrate High Scores

Catch people doing it right. Celebrate integrity, follow-through, consistency, and transparency. Recognize and reward behavior that builds trust—because what gets celebrated gets repeated.

Final Charge: Build a Trust-Rich Culture

Trust isn't built in strategy meetings. It's built in the hallway, the Zoom room, the 1:1, the late nights, and the last-minute pivots. It's built when things go wrong and you show up anyway.

In a trust-rich culture:

- People collaborate instead of compete.
- Sales move faster.
- Teams operate with confidence.
- Leaders get followership, not just authority.

This doesn't happen by accident. It happens because someone decides that trust is worth measuring, protecting, and prioritizing.

Let that someone be you.

My Story: Proof It's Possible

You've read the principles. Now here's the proof.

I lost my Trust Credit Score—hard. I lost my license, my position, and eventually my marriage. The people who once trusted me the most no longer did. And I had no one to blame but myself.

But I didn't give up.

I took full ownership. I rebuilt with consistent behavior. I didn't ask to be trusted again—I showed why I should be. Over time, I earned back the trust of leaders who had every reason to walk away. I rebuilt trust with my daughters after years of heartbreak. I started a new career in a city where no one knew me and built a reputation—one workshop, one meeting, one conversation at a time.

And today? The comeback is real.

I'm remarried to an incredible woman, and together we've built a blended family with five kids we love deeply. I've stepped into high levels of leadership and influence in both local and national organizations. I've been named a five-time award-winning Influencer—and yes, I was even voted the "Mayor" of my neighborhood.

Not because I had a perfect record. But because I lived the process I've shared in this book.

Behavior rebuilt what words alone never could.

Consistency rebuilt what a crash had broken.

And trust—real trust—came back stronger than ever.

Let's Wrap It With This:

- Everyone has a Trust Credit Score™.
- It's either helping you or hurting you.
- You can raise it—starting today.
- And once you do, it changes everything.

Trust isn't just the silent question in business.

It's the loudest signal in your success story.

Now go raise your score— **and help others do the same.**

About the Author

SCOTT CARLEY, known as "The Change Energizer," is a dynamic consultant, motivational speaker and Vistage Trusted Advisor who has been a catalyst for transformation across the globe. With an unwavering commitment to excellence, he has empowered thousands of leaders and CEOs in over 9 countries and all 50 states to turn their goals into tangible achievements.

Scott's unique approach has revitalized organizations, propelling them to the top 2% of their industries worldwide. He is known for his ability to break barriers and drive measurable success. As a two-term president of the National Speakers Association's Austin Chapter, Scott has influenced countless individuals and organizations, leaving an indelible mark on the business world.

Scott is a native Texan from Austin. He and his wife, Carol, have a blended family of five incredible adult children. In his downtime, Scott enjoys touring the Texas Hill Country on his Indian Roadmaster Limited motorcycle.

His most requested keynotes include:
Can I Trust You? The Silent Question Everyone Is Asking

LinkedIn Profile

https://www.linkedin.com/in/scarley

Instagram

https://www.instagram.com/sacarley/

YouTube

https://www.youtube.com/c/ScottCarley

X

https://x.com/SACarley

Get Energized

5 WAYS TO WORK WITH SCOTT CARLEY

Do You Want Scott to Speak at Your Conference or Event?

For associations, company-wide events, or keynotes

ConferenceEnergizer.com

Do You Want Scott to Speak at Your Leadership Retreat?

For executive and senior leadership off-sites

RetreatEnergizer.com

Do You Want Scott to Build a Trust Culture in Your Company?

For organizations that want on-site consulting,

training or cultural transformation

TrustCertifiedTeams.com

Do You Want to Get Certified as a
Trust Credit Score™ Facilitator?

For coaches, facilitators, consultants, and HR leaders

TrustCultureCertification.com

Do You Want to Listen to the Get Energized Podcast?

For weekly inspiration, trust insights, and real conversations with leaders who are making it happen

GetEnergizedPodcast.com

www.ingramcontent.com/pod-product-compliance
Lightning Source LLC
Chambersburg PA
CBHW050732150626
46551CB00038B/1018